CONTENTS

Fleet in Focus: Elder Dempster postwar
   (part 3) *Andrew Bell*   2
Record reviews   15
Railway steamers serving France, 1878-1952
   (part 2) *John de S. Winser*   16
Putting the Record straight   29
Grand Union (Shipping) Ltd.
   Roy Fenton and Alan Faulkner   30
Bosun's Locker   44
Robertson follow up   46
Sources and acknowledgements   48
The Clipper family of reefer vessels (part 3)
   Tony Breach   49
Elder Dempster in colour   60
Funnel and flag of Grand
   Union (Shipping) Ltd.   64

Ships in Focus Publications

Correspondence and editorial:
Roy Fenton
18 Durrington Avenue
London SW20 8NT
020 8879 3527
rfenton@rfenton.demon.co.uk

Orders and photographic:
John & Marion Clarkson
18 Franklands, Longton
Preston PR4 5PD
01772 612855
shipsinfocus@btinternet.com

Printed by Amadeus Press Ltd.,
Cleckheaton, Yorkshire.
Designed by Hugh Smallwood, John Clarkson and Roy Fenton.

SHIPS IN FOCUS RECORD
ISBN 978-1-901703-95-5

SUBSCRIPTION RATES FOR RECORD

Readers can start their subscription with any issue, and are welcome to backdate it to receive previous issues.

	3 issues	4 issues
UK	£24	£31
Europe (airmail)	£26	£34
Rest of the world (surface mail)	£26	£34
Rest of the world (airmail)	£31	£41

SHIPS IN FOCU
July 2(

The Ships in Focus Photographic Offer in interest, and all the feedback we have had from customers suggests that the digital photographs they received fully met their expectations. We had a few minor teething problems, which meant that the majority of the orders were not despatched until about six weeks after the closing date. We feel sufficiently encouraged to make another offer, this time for aerial views of ships photographed in Far Eastern waters, from negatives which we believe have not been offered before.

We are pleased that publishers have begun to send books for review in 'Record': previously we have simply chosen available titles which appeared to be of interest to readers. We will continue to be selective in our choice of what to review, knowing that space in each issue is rather precious.

'Putting the Record straight' is relatively short this month, but this does not mean we are lacking correspondence (as witness the response to the puzzle photographs published in 'Bosun's Locker'). Andrew Bell's articles on Elder Dempster (which are due to be concluded with an article on the mail ships in 'Record' 50) have generated unprecedented interest. It is our policy not to publish any letters on a multi-part feature until that feature has been concluded. The intention is to avoid anything which might smack of criticism of an author alongside his work. Not that the letters about Andrew's articles are critical: they overwhelmingly include additional detail or corroboration of Andrew's writing. If you have commented on these articles, you can expect to see the matter covered in 'Record' 51.

Needless to say, the next and fiftieth edition of 'Record' will be something of a milestone, and we have been busy planning its content. There will be extra colour, whilst the editors intend to indulge themselves modestly by covering subjects dear to their hearts, but which we also think readers will enjoy. If all goes to plan, it will be sent out early in November.

John Clarkson   Roy Fenton

July 2011

Canterbury of 1929: see page 19. *[J. and M. Clarkson]*

The sixth member of the F class, the last to be designed by Elder Dempster, *Fian* is outward bound lightly loaded but with a full complement of vehicles on deck. *[Fotoflite incorporating Skyfotos]*

ELDER DEMPSTER POST WAR Part 3

Andrew Bell

By 1960 Britain's withdrawals from its colonial empire had become commonplace events. Members of the royal family were flying to distant parts of the world to lend their dignified munificent presence to yet another Union flag being hauled down at the appointed midnight hour. By and large the British commercial investments in these colonies used their corporate foresight to plan for the coming era of 'freedom and justice', two features that all too often were diluted soon thereafter. With administrative independence, and emerging into Commonwealth status, Ghana, Nigeria, Sierra Leone and The Gambia made the change in 1957, 1960, 1961 and 1965 respectively. Regional bodies of the empire and their services were ended: out went a common currency, a central produce marketing corporation, a shared education examination system and a pan-national airline that linked them economically. In came those status symbols of a 'new nation', first amongst which was usually a national shipping line.

The British lines of the West African Lines Freight Conference, appreciating that flag discrimination would mean that the reservation of paying staple cargoes might be denied to them, lost no time in co-founding, and managing, the new national lines and readily admitted them to the Conference. Before the region-wide concepts of common services and investments were eliminated by rising nationalism, Ghana had proposed a joint shipping company with Nigeria in 1957 but, with no response, set up their own State Shipping Corporation – Black Star Line. Having lost out in managing this to Israel's expansionist Zim Line, Elder Dempster were not going to be sidelined in Nigeria. When in 1959 the Nigerian National Shipping Line was set up under the burgeoning talent of Donald H. Tod, Elder Dempster held 33%, with Palm Line 16% and the Federal government 51%. To do this, it helped that Elder Dempster had created a preferred status for themselves as, together with BOAC, and in partnership with the Nigerian government, they had founded Nigerian Airways in 1958. The subsequent histories of the national shipping companies ruined by avaricious civil servants, corrupt politicians and outright bad management, are well known (for Black Star see 'Record' 38; for Nigerian National 'Record' 41 and 42).

Preparing for a fever of nationalism, Elder Dempster had, as early as 1954, vested all their numerous fleet support activities and valuable property assets in West Africa in separate local companies in all of which, until 1972, they maintained sole ownership. This move, initiated by John H. Joyce, was to pay-off in both senses. The commercial advantage of maintaining a once-large Lagos-based fleet of coasters came to an end in 1962 as the steam locomotives on Ghana's and Nigeria's railways substituted coal for oil and, at the same time, the Nigerian Produce (Export) Marketing Board ceased to pay a supplementary freight charge on feeder services from the Niger Delta's 'Creek' ports. In various undeveloped ports lighterage fleets remained necessary: the riverine Cross River two-way service in Eastern Nigeria and West Cameroon plied on, and that microcosm of the mail boats, the Calabar Ferry Service, carrying 500,000 passengers a year on a 16-mile strategic route, continued with little notice and produced substantial profits.

The F class
With an active and forward-thinking technical department at head office in India Buildings, Liverpool, there was seldom a time when there was not the next class of ships for adding to the fleet on naval architect George Hunter's drawing board. So it was that, on 7th September 1961, Mrs. G. Payne, daughter of John H. Joyce, named the *Fourah Bay* and the ship was launched from Scott's yard at Greenock. Named after Sierra Leone's university college – the oldest in West Africa – the *Fourah Bay* was the lead ship of a class of six which were the last in Elder Dempster's history to be designed in-house specifically for the company's West African trade. One of the parameters that shaped the F class was an ability to serve the valuable and growing trade between Britain and Angola. At the time Angola had been a Portuguese colony since 1575 and much resembled what California must have been like when the Spanish arrived in the 16th century: it had rich soil, abundant water, mineral wealth, a sparse population and a temperate climate. Crossing the southern prairies of Angola was the British-owned Benguela Railway which carried over 100,000 tonnes of copper a year and provided the mines and smelting ventures of Zambia and Katanga (then in Zaire) an outlet to the world's markets. The natural harbour at Lobito was the western terminus of the Benguela Railway.

The F class were designed to be able to carry just over 8,000 tonnes on a loaded draught of 25 feet. Whilst this was 2,000 tonnes less than the D class, it meant that they could load a heavy bottom-stowed consignment of copper and the balance of northbound cargo from the rest of West Africa, and sail for the UK or Europe, loaded down to their marks. They also had four of their six deep tanks in number 3 hold in which, unusually, there was no 'tween deck. It was expected at the time of their being built that this was to enable them to easily carry large items of capital equipment which included double decker buses as southbound cargo: this proved wrong and hoistable car decks were later fitted.

A trend at the time was to specify that the midships accommodation structure be constructed of aluminium which, with a total weight of 70 tonnes, was 100 tonnes less than the conventional method of using steel. Another leap of confidence was the installation of a five-cylinder RD76 Sulzer main engine that produced 6,600 BHP and a service speed of 16 knots making them the fastest ships in the Elder Dempster fleet. These Sulzers were the company's first, and in service are remembered as being very satisfactory. The habitability features of each successive class improved on the previous one. On the Fs it was an expensive but satisfactory fitting and performance of a Carrier air conditioning plant, plus a sizeable swimming pool flush with the boat deck aft, and for the first time a spacious twin-bedded owner's suite.

The *Fourah Bay* replaced the *Obuasi* as the company's cadet training ship. No seamen were carried which meant that the 22 cadets could be accommodated in two-berth cabins, all amidships. As the cadets had the use of the officers' attractive lounge and bar across the after end of the promenade deck, what would have been the deck ratings' recreation room was fitted out as the cadets' study. The ship carried an extra chief officer, designated as the cadets' training officer. In the early 1960s Elder Dempster were serious about training their future officers, not only as navigators but also engineers and as purser-caterers. To facilitate this a shore establishment close to Riversdale Technical College, River House was built at Aigburth, a Liverpool suburb. Right from the start the best of the *Obuasi's* traditions were transferred to the brand new *Fourah Bay* and she was known as a happy ship. This was to the credit of John Smallwood – a retired Royal Navy captain – and Malcolm Bruce Glasier – the company's ships' husband, with their collective imaginative and sustained interest. This was manifest in ensuring that the cadets, who each spent not more than two successive voyages manning the *Fourah Bay,* saw something of Africa beyond the confines of the tumultuous ports at which the ship called.

With the withdrawal of the passenger ship *Accra* in November 1967, the resulting gap in the fortnightly mail boat service that operated on a six-week round voyage schedule between Liverpool and Lagos, was filled by the *Fourah Bay.* Not by coincidence this followed what Union Castle with Safmarine were doing on the South African mail service between 1967 and 1977. One reason for using the *Fourah Bay*, and not one of the E class trio, was so that the cadets' individual academic training schedules could be run to definite dates. Her cargo carrying capacity was 80% more than the two remaining mail boats but this was the dawning era of unit loads particularly in the form of pallets. This meant that the *Fourah Bay* could easily carry more freight but handle it within the set dates of the whole schedule: drop stow through five hatches helped. The most significant development was

that the net profit from each 42-day voyage of *Fourah Bay* often approached £30,000. To put this figure in the context of 1968, a top-end Rover 2000 that was being carried to Nigeria had a 'free-onboard' value of around £1,000.

The second of the F class was the *Falaba,* an exact sister ship but without the adaptations for being crewed by cadets, delivered in June 1962. The remaining four ships were built by Lithgows who, having built all the K class for Hendersons, were well known to Elder Dempster. The *Forcados* was the first of the quartet to be delivered in November 1963, followed by the *Fulani* in January 1964, the *Freetown* in February 1964 and last of all, with a name never previously used by the company, the *Fian,* in April 1964. The cost of the *Fian* was £2,200,000 which, for comparison, was around the same price as BOAC were paying for one of their new VC 10 airliners that came into service on the London to Lagos route in April 1962.

The only difference between the Scotts-built pair and the Lithgows' quartet was a larger heavy lift derrick with a safe-working-load of up to 80-tonnes (the earlier two were 50-tonnes SWL) on the forward side of the bipod mainmast, and a 30-tonne SWL derrick on the after side, and another 30-tonnes derrick serving number 4 hatch on the after mast. The four bipod masts that Scotts had put on the *Egori* in 1956 were rated as being a success worth repeating and so each of the F class had three. With so much cargo handling gear attached to the mainmast, the Lithgows' ships were completed with a signal mast over the bridge whose appearance was spoilt by its appearing to be propped up by the funnel.

Ocean Fleets

Having become a publicly quoted company in 1965, Alfred Holt-Blue Funnel Line was re-named Ocean Transport and Trading and terms were agreed to take over Liner Holdings – Elder Dempster's financial parent – from 1964 and which came into effect on 1st January 1965. It has become folklore amongst the staff afloat and ashore that Ocean had long held a 35% shareholding in Liner Holdings in order to get their hands on the latter's cash. The financial records show that there is some truth in this assertion. Liner Holdings' reserves and retained profit had grown from £19,000,000 in

The cadet ship *Fourah Bay*, first of the F class. *[J. and M. Clarkson]*

In September 1977 *Freetown* was under the Dutch flag, using her own gear to discharge hardwood logs into lighters. *[Ships in Focus]*

1956 to £36,000,000 in 1965: it was that year that the 'four knights' of the four main British shipping companies formed Overseas Containers Ltd. in which Ocean initially had a 19.5% shareholding. A direct result of the takeover was a rationalisation by both Blue Funnel and Elder Dempster of ship operations, staffing, training and management resulting in what was to become a prominent identity in the form of Ocean Fleets.

In a defensive move to block a London-based conglomerate with wide ambitions in Africa, in 1965 Elder Dempster bought the shipping interests of the Liverpool merchants John Holt, who had a shipping subsidiary, Guinea Gulf Line. As all four ships that came with the acquisition were steam powered, they were not suitable for integration into the Elder Dempster all-diesel-engined fleet and no time was lost in disposing of them with only one, the *Mary Holt* (5,577/1959), making one round voyage to West Africa under

Elder Dempster and she duly had engine trouble. For reasons of taxation and Conference membership Guinea Gulf, as a company, was kept trading although the management was taken over by Ocean Fleets from T. and J. Brocklebank.

Funded by Elder Dempster, Hendersons built two ships for their long-established UK-Burma trade. This pair were the *Bhamo* of 1957 and the *Pegu* of 1961: both came from Lithgows and the *Pegu* was regarded as being the fourth of the three-ship Henderson D class ('Record' 48). Both ships had deep tanks that were intended more for water ballast than for oil or latex. Flag-state preference and the torpid nature of Burma's economy caused the cessation of Henderson's long and proud services to the country in 1966, resulting in both ships being employed in the West African trades until their disposal in 1979 and 1980. As Nigeria's export of vegetable oils trailed off as domestic demand rose in the 1970s, this pair's lack of small tanks was not

Henderson's *Pegu* (5,764/1961) underwent a number of transfers but by the time of this photograph dated March 1979 she was formally owned by Guinea Gulf Line Ltd. and is in their colours. She was sold in October 1980, initially simply renamed *Regu* by an Isle of Man-based outfit. Subsequent names were *Joelle* (1981) and *Nicol Mylo* (1982), before she was sold to Taiwan breakers in 1983. *[J. and M. Clarkson]*

Bhamo (5,932/1957) entered Henderson's Burma service in this old-established company's dignified but restrained livery of black funnel and black hull with a white line separating the red boot topping. These elegant hull colours are apparent in the top photograph, whilst in the lower left *Bhamo* sports an Elder Dempster funnel. In the lower right photograph, showing *Bhamo* docking at Liverpool on 12th April 1975, she is in Guinea Gulf Line colours and has lost the white hull line. In April 1979 she was sold to Hong Kong owners who changed her name simply to *Bhamot* and loaded her for the Far East. She arrived at a Taiwan scrap yard in July. Note her shapely stem. *[J. and M. Clarkson; Roy Fenton collection; J. and M. Clarkson]*

the operational problem that it might have been ten years previously. Henderson's last two passenger cargo ships, *Prome* (7,043/1937) and *Salween* (7,063/1938), had been withdrawn in 1962 and were never used on Elder Dempster's West African services.

By 1972 the combined Elder Dempster and Guinea Gulf fleet of cargo ships totalled 37 vessels but they were becoming relatively elderly with an average age of 13 years. With more than half the southbound trade to West Africa being handled through Lagos' Apapa Quays and rapid economic development based on crude oil exports, the whole make-up and volume of Nigeria's cargo trades was changing. Not seen for many previous decades, berthing delays became common place at the less efficient West African ports. At its most extreme phase, this was manifested as hundreds of ships full of bagged cement cargoes anchored in Lagos Roads (see 'The Great Cement Armada' in 'Record' 38) as a result of corrupt Nigerian Army officers getting their hands freely on letters of credit (issued on c.i.f. terms), pocketing the resulting large commissions (in hard currency) and abandoning the transactions, the ships and their cargoes.

New S class

An adjunct of the West German chancellor Willie Brandt's Oostpolitik diplomacy was a facility to finance West German ship owners who ordered ships from Polish yards who were building for operators within the Soviet empire. Amongst those placing orders was H. Schuldt of Hamburg who initially contracted for four ships from Stocznia Szczecinska to be built to a German design: the third and fourth were not needed and, through the labours of John Robertson a wily Scot and an Elder Dempster director, Ocean bought them. The number eventually grew to five ships: these became the new S class. The third of the six, originally intended to be named *Sobo*, was taken by Nigerian National Shipping Line as *River Hadeja* amidst a spending spree that was ultimately to lead to their demise. The cost of each ship was around £6,000,000 with the actual owners being a leasing company associated with the Midland Bank – they were never owned by Ocean. This was a practise that was to become common. A condition of the West-East financing was that the ships had to be delivered to Schuldt and then sold to the British owner. Bizarrely, the transfer was effected at sea as the ships emerged into the North Sea from the Kiel Canal. With all the accommodation down aft, seafarers hardened by many years at sea and used to living amidships suffered sea sickness that they had never known before.

The S class came into service from 1973 onwards and stimulated the development of the long-trialled plans to expand the Elder Dempster–Palm Line African Container Express service, as each ship could carry 795 TEU. The staple southbound trade was being eroded by a motley collection of non-Conference operators and to counter this attack the liner operators pooled their ships and tonnages under a common brand name, UKWAL (UK West Africa Line). Within ten years the S class was too small so they were superceded by the seven-strong Ocean Standard Liner class – all with Blue Funnel M names. In service these were too large and too expensive to operate in West Africa. It could be said that they were over-designed: their cargo gear was complicated and they had a reputation for being difficult to handle in confined waterways. Attempts to use Blue Funnel's ships designed for the Far East routes in West Africa revealed that they had a host of limitations. For example, a Henderson K class ship could lift 4,000 tonnes over the Niger River Delta's Escravos bar on a draught of 16 feet, whilst a Blue Funnel *Anchises* class (built between 1947 and 1957) was empty of any cargo at the same draught.

As Peter Davies graphically describes in his definitive history of Elder Dempster Lines 'The Trade Makers', West African trades were becoming more orientated towards the Far East and North and South America and with it, and as a shrinking minor part of the Ocean Group becoming a conglomerate, came the demise of Elder Dempster.

The first of the Ocean Standard Liners, *Maron*, was completed by Scott's Shipbuilding and Engineering Co. Ltd. at Greenock in 1980. Although launch photos show a black top to her funnel, indicating Blue Funnel colours, she made her maiden voyage from Liverpool on Elder Dempster's West African service. She is seen in Elder Dempster colours, but for the purposes of this article she is regarded as one of many Blue Funnel ships which painted up Elder Dempster colours – in some cases for just one voyage – in the dying years of the West African service. *[Fotoflite incorporating Skyfotos/Roy Fenton collection]*

FOURAH BAY

Scott's Shipbuilding and Engineering Co. Ltd., Greenock, 1961; 7,704g, 465 feet 2SCSA 5-cyl. oil engine by Sulzer Brothers Ltd., Winterthur, Switzerland
Fourah Bay was launched on 7th September 1961. The middle photograph (on the New Waterway) shows her as completed in December 1962, with a radar mast separated from her funnel, and forecastle and poop bulwarks painted white. Later, as the bottom photograph shows, the radar mast was attached to the funnel, which has grown a rather ugly tripod mast, probably fabricated from surplus derricks, presumably to support aerials and a signal hoist. The white half rounds have gone and masts are brown.

She was sold in January 1978, and over the next six years ran as *Magda Josefina* under Bermudan registry, *Alexander's Faith* under the Greek flag, and as the Cypriot-flag *Lemina*. Breakers at Gadani Beach took her in March 1984 and set to work within weeks. *[Roy Fenton collection; World Ship Society Ltd.]*

FALABA

Scott's Shipbuilding and Engineering Co. Ltd., Greenock, 1962; 7,703g, 465 feet
Sulzer-type 2SCSA 5-cyl. oil engine by Scott's Shipbuilding and Engineering Co. Ltd., Greenock
Launched from Scott's yard on 9th January 1962 by Miss Hilary Muirhead, daughter of Elder Dempster's long-serving Freight Director, *Falaba* was externally indistinguishable from *Fourah Bay*, despite the latter's cadet ship role. *Falaba* underwent the same modifications, and is shown before (in August 1965) and after changes to her signal mast/funnel.

Parallels with her exact sister persisted after her sale, and she was part of the same January 1978 deal which saw her become *Leonor Maria* under Bermudan registry but with Mexican principals. She too went to Greece in June 1980 as *Alexander's Trust*, with Gabriel Panayotides as her ultimate owner. Her final name, *City of Zug,* taken in 1983, suggests a Swiss connection, but she was managed in Piraeus and registered in Limassol. She arrived at Chittagong for breaking up in September 1984.
[J. and M. Clarkson; B. Reeves]

FORCADOS

Lithgows Ltd., Port Glasgow, 1963; 7,689g, 465 feet
Sulzer-type 2SCSA 5-cyl. oil engine by Fairfield-Rowan Ltd., Glasgow.
First of four F class from Lithgows' Port Glasgow yard, *Forcados* was launched on 24th March by Mrs Gwen Lane, wife of Elder Dempster's Chairman, Frank Lane. The upper photograph, taken at a US port and with what looks like ice damage to her boot topping forward, clearly shows the extra heavy lift derricks on the main and after masts which was the main difference from the Scotts' pair. The signal mast has also been redesigned and, from photographs of the other Lithgows-built examples, this appears not to have required modification during their Elder Dempster careers. In the lower photograph in the Malacca Straits she appears to be in Blue Funnel colours.

In 1975 *Forcados* was sold, with *Fulani,* to Cameroun Shipping Lines S.A. of Douala who renamed her *Cam Ayous.* In March 1981 she was sold to Greeks who renamed her *Copper Trader,* as which she was arrested for debt at Mombasa in October 1983. She was then fit only for scrap, and was towed to Karachi where demolition began immediately on her arrival in November 1984.
[Ships in Focus; J. and M. Clarkson]

FULANI

Lithgows Ltd., Port Glasgow, 1964;
7,689g, 465 feet
Sulzer-type 2SCSA 5-cyl. oil engine by
Fairfield-Rowan Ltd., Glasgow.
Fulani was launched on 27th June
1963 by Mrs T. Kennan, wife of the
company's Accountant. The upper two
photographs (the second taken on the
Mersey) serve to illustrate that the only
change during her relatively short Elder
Dempster career was to the painting of
her forecastle, poop and masts.

Cameroun Shipping Lines
S.A. renamed her *Cam Azobe* in
December 1975. In 1981 she was sold
to become *Cotton Trader* for the same
Greek principals who took the former
Forcados, known as Manta Shipping
Co. Ltd. of Liberia, notwithstanding their
headquarters being in Piraeus. For
these owners she was no more fortunate
than *Copper Trader,* as in July 1983 her
crew abandoned her when she caught
fire following an explosion in number
4 hold during a voyage from Dubai to
Aden. She went aground, but was
towed off in February 1984, languishing
at Djibouti until November 1984 when
she was delivered to Gadani Beach for
breaking up. *[Roy Fenton collection;J.*
and M. Clarkson]

FREETOWN

Lithgows Ltd., Port Glasgow, 1964;
7,689g, 465 feet
Sulzer-type 2SCSA 5-cyl. oil engine by
Fairfield-Rowan Ltd., Glasgow.
Freetown was originally intended for
Henderson's Burmese services. When
she was launched on 19th September
1963 by Mrs Margo Chalcroft (wife of
a company manager in West Africa)
the port of registry painted on her stern
was Glasgow rather than Liverpool,
an error that was amended prior to
registration in February 1964. This
may have been an omen that she was
to undergo more internal transfers than
any other of the F class ships, starting
with a 1967 move from Elder Dempster
(lower middle photograph, July 1966
on the Thames) to Guinea Gulf Line
Ltd. (bottom photo, 1968, also on the
Thames). In 1972 she went to Blue
Funnel's Dutch branch, Nederlandsche
Stoomvaart Maatschappij 'Ocean' N.V.,
who repainted her funnel blue, even if
they did not rename her or remove the
Elder Dempster bow crest (top photo,
overleaf).

Whilst at Middlesbrough in
May 1978 she was sold to two London
Greek owners who renamed her
Panseptos under the Greek flag. Just
over two years later she moved to
Singapore registry for Madame Dolly
Seah as *Cherry Ruby,* as which she
was photographed in decent condition

at Singapore in March 1981 (middle photo). However, things were not so calm on board as during April it was reported that there was a shooting during a mutiny, and this was followed by fire on board, the aftermath of which can be seen in the bottom photograph. Picked up off Penang by the tug *Smit New York* (1,826/1977), she was towed back to Singapore and from there made her inevitable way to the breakers, arriving at Chittagong in January 1982. *[Roy Fenton collection (2); Fotoflite incorporating Skyfotos; Roy Kittle; J. and M. Clarkson]*

FIAN

Lithgows Ltd., Port Glasgow, 1964; 7,689g, 465 feet
Sulzer-type 2SCSA 5-cyl. oil engine by Fairfield-Rowan Ltd., Glasgow.

Fian was also intended for Burmese routes, and she too had 'Glasgow' on her stern when launched on 15th October 1963 by Mrs. Barbara Lucas, wife of West Coast Manager John Lucas.

Elder Dempster mast colours, seen in the first two photographs, gave way to Ocean brown, as in the aerial view bottom (see also page 2).

The South East Asia Shipping Co. Private Ltd. of Bombay took *Fian* in 1975, renaming her *Mahapriya*. Ten years later she was broken up at her home port of Bombay, work commencing in April 1985. *[Ships in Focus; J. and M. Clarkson; Fotoflite incorporating Skyfotos]*

SHONGA

Stocznia Szczecinska A. Warskiego, Szczecin, Poland, 1973; 5,677g, 145.7 metres
Sulzer-type 2SCSA 6-cyl. oil engine by H. Cegielski, Poznan, Poland.

Owners of *Shonga*, as with the most of the S class, were the finance company Midland Montagu Leasing (U.K.) Ltd. who leased her to Elder Dempster. Nevertheless, she was launched by Mrs Peggy Ellerton, wife of the Chairman of Elder Dempster Lines.

Following a period of lay-up in the River Fal, *Shonga* was sold in April 1984, subsequent names being *Aroma*, *Dona*, *Mariocean*, *Grand Liberty*, *Lotus Dawn*, *Lotus* and *Excelsior Luck*. She arrived at Guangzhou for breaking up in January 1997.

Shonga was photographed off Thameshaven on 15th August 1983 from London & Rochester's coaster *Lodella*. *[V.H. Young and L.A. Sawyer]*

SHERBRO

Stocznia Szczecinska A. Warskiego, Szczecin, Poland, 1974; 5,677g, 145.88 metres
Sulzer-type 2SCSA 6-cyl. oil engine by H. Cegielski, Poznan, Poland.

Third of the name, *Sherbro* was also launched (on 15th December 1973) by an executive's lady, Mrs Mandy Earlam, wife of the Freight Director of Elder Dempster Lines.

Sale in 1984 (to the Singapore owners who also bought *Shonga*) was inevitably followed by multiple renamings, and ten are recorded: *Sherry, Rita, Mariland, Clara, Santa Clara I, Santa Mercedes, NGS Express, Prafita, Meng Yang,* and *Fong Dar*. She was broken up at Alang, India, where work began in March 1998. *[Fotoflite incorporating Skyfotos 257456]*

SOKOTO (opposite page, top photo)
Stocznia Szczecinska A. Warskiego, Szczecin, Poland, 1979; 5,560g, 145.01 metres
Sulzer-type 2SCSA 6-cyl. oil engine by H. Cegielski, Poznan, Poland.

Despite being officially delivered to H. Schuldt, and never owned by Elder Dempster, *Sokoto* was launched at Szczecin on 12th August 1978 by Mrs Penny Toosey, wife of the Director of Ocean Liners.

Sokoto began her maiden voyage for Elder Dempster from

Liverpool on 2nd April 1979. From May 1983 she was renamed *Bello Folawiyo* for charter to Nigerian Green Lines Ltd. of Lagos, reverting to *Sokoto* in 1984.

Sold along with four of her sisters in 1986, she first went to Venezuela as *General Urdaneta*. In 1992 she was sold again, becoming first *Meng Horng* and soon after, *Meng Kiat* under Singapore ownership. She was sold to breakers at Alang in 1998, but almost cheated them. On 3rd July the cable from her towing vessel broke in bad weather when she was 20 miles off Mumbai and *Meng Kiat* drifted ashore, only to be plundered by locals. It was not until December that she resumed her voyage to Alang.
[Fotoflite incorporating Skyfotos/Roy Fenton collection]

SEKONDI (middle and bottom)
Stocznia Szczecinska A. Warskiego, Szczecin, Poland, 1979; 5,677g, 145.01 metres
Sulzer-type 2SCSA 6-cyl. oil engine by H. Cegielski, Poznan, Poland.
Sekondi was launched on 2nd December 1978 by Mrs F. Roby, wife of the Finance Manager of Ocean Liners. Confusingly for those choosing illustrations for this feature, *Sekondi* was also renamed *Bello Folawiyo* for charter to Nigerian Green Lines Ltd., this time from July to December 1985, as in the bottom photo.

Sale in 1986 was followed by a string of renamings, to *Deo Juvente*, then *Merkur America*, *EAL Opal*, *Berlioz*, *Wing Son* and *Jaami*. On 26th December 2004 the Bangladesh-

owned *Jaami* was driven against the breakwater at Colombo as a result of a tsunami following an earthquake at Aceh. She was refloated in January

2005 but declared a total loss.
[Fotoflite incorporating Skyfotos/J. and M. Clarkson collection; Fotoflite incorporating Skyfotos 321632]

SAPELE

Stocznia Szczecinska A. Warskiego, Szczecin, Poland, 1980; 5,657g, 145.88 metres Sulzer-type 2SCSA 6-cyl. oil engine by H. Cegielski, Poznan, Poland.

Sponsor of *Sapele* at her launch on 7th September 1979 was Mrs Anne Sykes, wife of the Director of UK/West Africa Trade for Ocean Liners.

Sapele was chartered several times during the early 1980s, first by the British Ministry of Defence for the Falkland Islands work in June 1982 and in February 1983 by Curnow Shipping Ltd. for a voyage to Ascension Island carrying prefabricated buildings for the RAF base. Later in 1983 she was chartered by Lamport and Holt Line Ltd. for a South American voyage.

Subsequent to her sale to French owners in 1986, *Sapele* was variously named *Antilles*, *Saint Pierre*, *Astra Sea*, *Bulk Trader* and *Senja Fjord* before being broken up in July 2010. She is seen as *Saint Pierre* (middle) and as *Astra* Sea with a full deck cargo of vehicles and plant (bottom). *[Fotoflite incorporating Skyfotos/ Roy Fenton collection; Fotoflite incorporating Skyfotos214136 and 276792]*

14

RECORD REVIEWS

ULSTER'S SHIPS & QUAYSIDES: A PHOTOGRAPHIC RECORD
Robert Anderson and Ian Wilson
200 x 240mm softback of 128 pages
Published by Colourpoint Books, Newtownards, 2011 at £8.99

This is the authors' second volume of photographs depicting the many and varied aspects of shipping around Ulster: a similar volume in 1990 included photographs taken up to 1945. The present volume covers the period since the Second World War, but like its predecessor it records many vanished scenes, such have been the changes since 1945.

The coverage is certainly thorough. All ports, harbours and quays of any consequence appear to have been covered, including many which no longer see a vessel. The ships depicted vary from steam coasters, through fishing craft to high speed ferries and cruise liners. There are naval craft, dredgers, local ferries and excursion vessels, tugs and even an oil rig, all pictured in the context of local port facilities – the rig being depicted in Harland and Wolff's yard. A number of accidents are featured, including the *Nellie M*, sunk by IRA bombs in Lough Foyle.

The authors have limited themselves to about one hundred words for each caption so, whilst they have succeeded in putting each view into its geographical or historical context, there is usually no room for the histories of the vessels depicted. A welcome feature, given the obscurity of some of the locations, is a map of the province of Ulster, indicating where each photograph was taken, from Carlingford northwards and westwards around the coast to Donegal.

As the authors acknowledge, the quality of the images available to them varies from good to acceptable, but they have been chosen largely because of their historical interest, a sentiment with which any compiler of illustrated books will agree. Of the 120 images, 16 are in colour, and come from a wide variety of photographers. Given the variability of image quality, reproduction is usually good, and at £8.99 the printers have done well to produce a very worthwhile book at a very reasonable price.

PALM OIL AND SMALL CHOP
John Goble
170 x 240mm softback of 224 pages
Published by Whittles Publishing, Dunbeath, 2011 at £16.99

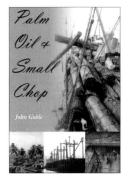

The best books by seafarers succeed in combining a personal narrative retaining the reader's interest with a vivid description of a trade and a way of life which have both passed. John Goble's account of his life in three companies trading between the UK and West Africa is certainly one of the best this reviewer has read. Like the writings of Captain A.W. Kinghorn, this book provides just enough of the story of the author's career to provide a background to his gripping account of what life was like for a ship's officer in this unique and demanding trade, and how it changed completely over his career.

Too often, those writing such accounts tend to assume that the story of their ascent from cadet to captain is uniquely fascinating, whereas John Goble is selective in telling his story, giving the reader just enough to appreciate the day-to-day problems faced by officers of various seniorities. And problems there were in spades in this trade, from the almost incessant risk of pilfering cargo, through the personal trading habits of seafarers from Nigeria or Ghana, to the corruption and growing inefficiency endemic to many West African port facilities. Added to this were unique geographical challenges, including working cargo offshore at the last remaining surf port, navigating mighty tropical rivers such as the Congo, and ensuring that the packages of cargo which were often being unloaded and loaded simultaneously by not always skilled labour were not only stowed correctly but would be accessible at their destined port.

The author worked successively for Elder, Dempster, Nigerian National and Palm Line and, although he does not set out to overtly criticise any of his employees, his account brings out much which is of interest to the historian of these lines. Indeed, as the author acknowledges, some small sections of the book have appeared in 'Record' as commentaries on the histories of Nigerian National and Palm. But it is West Africa, in all its fascinating richness and at times poverty, seen from the bridge and offices of a cargo liner, that is the focus of this book, and one doubts whether it could have been better observed or recorded.

The format of the book is familiar from what appear to be an endless stream of largely pictorial books from a string of publishers in Gloucestershire. However, production qualities are far better, including the editing and proof reading, as well as the reproduction of the small cluster of black and white photographs. Perhaps for this reason, this paper back is not cheap, but its content is all but priceless.

CLOSING DOWN SAIL
Martin Benn
A4 hardback of over 200 pages
Published by the author, 2011 at £22.00

Martin Benn has spent thirty years researching the many small British sailing ships which survived into the twentieth century, and this book is the result. It comprises an alphabetical listing of over three thousand coastal smacks, schooners and ketches with date and place of build and name of builder, rig, official number, tonnages and dimensions, port of registry, final owners and fate. Sources are largely the primary ones: Custom House Registers, plus crew lists, wreck and casualty returns compiled by the Board of Trade, Lloyd's Register and the publishers of 'Lloyd's Lists'. The author's upper tonnage limit is 400grt, and he has omitted fishing vessels and spritsail barges. As testimony to his thoroughness, a lengthy appendix catalogues vessels which appeared to be candidates for inclusion but proved upon further research to be what he calls 'red herrings', including schooner-rigged yachts, dumb barges, motor schooners and pilot and light vessels.

An introduction discusses why and how the data was compiled, and gives details of sources. The data on individual ships is set out very clearly in small but perfectly readable type. There are no photographs, but wisely, for what is a reference book, a hardback format has been chosen.

To call this book a tour-de force hardly does it justice. Even given its concentration on ships still registered in 1900, the book is likely to become the first resort for anyone researching coastal sail. Even if, like the reviewer, sailing vessels are not one's primary focus, for anyone with an interest in British coastal shipping 'Closing Down Sail' is a must-have reference work. If only every shipping researcher could complete his work in such a fashion!

Roy Fenton

RAILWAY STEAMERS SERVING FRANCE, 1878-1952
Part 2
John de S. Winser

PARIS 1913
Built for the London, Brighton and South Coast Railway by William Denny and Brothers, Dumbarton; 1,774gt, 293·5 feet
Two sets of geared steam turbines by Denny and Co., Dumbarton.
Designed for the Newhaven to Dieppe service, *Paris* achieved a trials speed of 24·765 knots over the measured mile and first reached Newhaven in July 1913. She was for a number of years regarded as the fastest vessel in the world in relation to her size, with a horse power listed as 14,000, in contrast to the 6,000 of her predecessor, the 1903-built *Brighton*. It would have been interesting to know to what extent business on the route would have been transformed, had the London, Brighton and South Coast Railway's 1911 plans to operate

a train ferry service been pursued. As it was, passenger numbers increased by 25% in September 1923, the first year of Southern Railway management, compared to the same month the previous year.

The photograph below shows *Paris* alongside the quay at Dieppe, prior to the open-sided areas of the promenade deck being enclosed and fitted with windows to provide enhanced passenger comfort. Severe gales, normally a feature of winter travel, can also occur at other times of the year, one such storm causing the steamer to sustain damage by striking Dieppe's East Pier at the end of a crossing on 21st August 1931. Listed as still capable of 23·2 knots, in 1933 *Paris* varied her previous routine by embarking on a programme of day excursions from

Brighton to Dieppe, a consistently profitable assignment which she took over when the 1900 *Arundel* was retired from railway service. In the six years to 1938, *Paris* completed 109 such round trips, carrying in excess of 34,000 excursionists. She was, however, due for replacement, so, in November 1939, the Southern Railway reserved the slipway vacated by their new Dover steamer *Invicta* but the plan was not acceptable to the French, who were already financing the construction of one cargo and two passenger vessels for the joint service. *Paris* was requisitioned on the very day the Second World War was declared and was bombed and sunk on 3rd June 1940, despite her prominent hospital carrier markings. *[A.M.S. Russell collection]*

BIARRITZ 1915 and MAID OF ORLEANS 1918 (opposite)
Built for the South Eastern and Chatham Railway by William Denny and Brothers, Dumbarton; 2,495gt (Biarritz), 2,384gt (Maid of Orleans), 341·2 feet
Four steam turbines single-reduction geared to two screw shafts by Denny and Co., Dumbarton.

Both ships would have been delivered by the end of August 1915 had First World War priorities not intervened. In consequence, *Maid of Orleans*, launched more than three years after her sister, was the first to enter commercial service, doing so between Dover and Calais on 1st June 1920. *Biarritz* made her maiden voyage on

the Folkestone to Boulogne route on 24th December 1921, after strikes had seriously delayed her post-war reconditioning. The 5th May 1923 saw *Biarritz* conveying King George V and Queen Mary across the Channel on their way to a state visit to Italy: flying the White Ensign and Admiralty flag at the fore and the Royal Standard at the main, the steamer left Dover for Calais with an escort of no fewer than nine Royal Navy destroyers.

The upper photograph below shows one of the two sister ships at Calais: at that time, the funnel colour was an economy-inspired black but this, in 1924, gave way to buff with black top, in accordance with the scheme adopted for the whole Southern Railway fleet. The boat deck and parts of the open-sided area of the deck below could at times become uncomfortably wet in rough weather, despite the provision of canvas side screens. This discomfort was aggravated by what the company described as the 'habit of passengers seemingly to make it a point of honour to over-weight themselves with hand baggage'. In an attempt to improve both ships in line with the new vessels introduced in 1925, major alterations were undertaken and the lower photograph of *Biarritz* leaving Boulogne shows the ship's appearance after the closing off of the open-sided areas of the awning deck, the lengthening of her funnels and the removal of their cowls.

Arriving at Boulogne from Folkestone on 9th October 1926, abnormal currents caused *Biarritz* to go aground and totally block the harbour entrance: with propeller, rudder and bottom damage, tugs finally freed her and brought her alongside the quay. In 1937 *Maid of Orleans* was one of the most heavily-worked vessels in the Strait of Dover fleet, completing no fewer than 613 Channel crossings. Sailings on the Folkestone to Boulogne route continued until 5th September 1939 for *Maid of Orleans* and for a further three days for *Biarritz*, before both vessels were requisitioned for Second World War service. The former vessel was lost on 28th June 1944 and, although *Biarritz* survived and was assigned post-war government duties, her condition made it uneconomic to refit her for commercial work and she was sold for demolition in 1949. *[A.M.S. Russell collection]*

DINARD and ST BRIAC 1924

Built for the Southern Railway by William Denny and Brothers Ltd., Dumbarton; 2,291gt, 316 feet

Four steam turbines single-reduction geared to two screw shafts by William Denny and Brothers Ltd., Dumbarton.

When ordering these two sister ships, the plan was that, for the purposes of comparison, one would run on oil fuel whilst the other would be a conventional coal-burner. In fact, both were completed with oil-fired boilers and became the first of their type to be so equipped. They were based at Southampton, with *Dinard* entering service on the 151-mile route to St Malo on 22nd July 1924 and *St Briac*,

seen in the first photograph, starting her maiden voyage to Le Havre that 3rd October. The completion of a new harbour enabled the overnight St Malo service, with which both steamers were mainly associated, to be changed from a tidal basis to a regular schedule, thereby preventing a repetition of occasions, as far back as 1893, when railway steamers had become trapped for over 12 hours, after the rise in tide failed to float them at departure time.

Because of a serious decline in passenger traffic to St Malo, at weekends in June 1932 *St Briac* commenced a programme of 'Short Cruises to France from 63/-' (£3.15p), with destinations including Rouen as

well as the normal range of railway ports. These cruises went on to attract over 12,000 passengers in the first four years, with the vessel later becoming the first of her type to be equipped with an open-air swimming pool.

After the outbreak of the Second World War, *St Briac* closed the direct St Malo service on 28th May 1940 and became a war loss by striking a British mine on 12th March 1942. *Dinard* survived damage from a German mine during the 1944 Normandy operations and was selected for a life-extending Tyneside conversion to a 1,765 gross ton car ferry to sail between Dover and Boulogne. Her internal and external appearance was

transformed, with the original sleeping accommodation for 354 replaced by space for 300 day passengers and 73 crane-loaded cars – 53 on the main deck and the remainder on the aft end of the promenade deck. Making a single daily round trip between 1st July and 9th October 1947, she carried 8,584 cars and over 25,000 passengers, uneventfully except on 18th July when dense fog prevented her entry into Dover Harbour for almost 15 hours. Fog was also a factor on 19th February 1950 when she hit Dover's Eastern Arm, twisting a four-foot section of her stem 40 degrees to port and totally crushing her starboard anchor.

Dinard is seen at the bottom of the opposite page in September 1952 after conversion. That summer she combined her Dover to Boulogne schedule with a once-weekly round trip on her pre-war Southampton to St Malo route but, with an average load of fewer than 27 cars per sailing, this arrangement was understandably never repeated. The photograph to the right is of Dinard at Boulogne after the provision of stern access to the car deck had eliminated the previous crane handling requirement. This alteration enabled the ship to perform the official opening of the Dover Eastern Docks ferry terminal on 30th June 1953, thereby heralding the start of full 'drive-on, drive-off' service. The Dover ramp made news again on 25th August 1956, when Dinard crushed her stern against it, injuring four of her 213 passengers and necessitating the crane discharge of their vehicles. Despite the fact that the vessel had already exceeded her planned lifespan by nine years, in October 1958 her railway service ended only to give way to a new career under the Finnish flag. *[Author's collection; J. and M. Clarkson; A.M.S. Russell collection]*

ISLE OF THANET and MAID OF KENT 1925
Built for the Southern Railway by William Denny and Brothers Ltd., Dumbarton; 2,664gt, 329·5 feet
Four steam turbines single-reduction geared to two screw shafts by William Denny and Brothers Ltd., Dumbarton.
CANTERBURY 1929
Built for the Southern Railway by William Denny and Brothers Ltd., Dumbarton; 2,912gt, 329.6 feet
Four steam turbines single-reduction geared to two screw shafts by William Denny and Brothers Ltd., Dumbarton.
In September 1923 alone, passenger numbers on the routes to Calais (from Dover) and to Boulogne (from both Dover and Folkestone) had increased by 22% compared with the same month the previous year and the

resultant overcrowding prompted the Southern Railway's order for two new passenger steamers. Named *Isle of Thanet*, the first ship started on the Dover-Calais route on 24th July 1925 and the photograph below of one of the two sister ships backing into Calais shows that the open-sided awning deck, featured in previous vessels, had been largely discarded, with the interior passenger space being further enlarged by combining the uptakes into a single funnel.

Less than a month after her delivery, the second vessel, *Maid of Kent*, encountered fog outside Calais on 21st November 1925: carried by the tide against the western pier, she steamed out again, only to collide with the eastern pier on her next attempt. The photograph to the right, taken on 19th March 1926, shows the bows of *Maid of Kent* buckled right back, after a strong tide had carried her on to Dover's southern breakwater, an accident for which her master was severely censured.

Early in 1928, the Southern Railway ordered yet another addition to its fleet, to provide the Dover to Calais connection of an accelerated 6 hours 35 minute London to Paris premium

service to be called the 'Golden Arrow'. Given the name *Canterbury*, the new steamer was an improved version of the 1925 ships, her main external recognition features being her stern shape and bulwarks and the raised davit stowage of the six after lifeboats, as can be seen from the photograph above showing the vessel gliding stern-first into Boulogne in her later years. *Canterbury* entered service on 15th May 1929 catering solely for the 250-300 using the 'Golden Arrow' Pullman train, non-premium travellers being provided with a separate steamer for their Channel crossing. In 1930 *Canterbury* made a total of 621 single Channel crossings but by early 1931 the economic situation dictated that she should be adapted so that all classes of passenger could be

accommodated in the same ship.

In 1934, the stem, bow rudder and plating of *Isle of Thanet* were affected by a collision with the pier at Dover on 21st November and, on 14th February 1937, whilst leaving Boulogne in dense evening fog, she sustained further bow damage and injured eight of her 198 passengers by striking a breakwater under construction just outside the port. Exactly two weeks later, a tremendous snow storm swept the Channel: *Maid of Kent*, with 77 passengers, failed to reach Boulogne at the expected time, so tugs were sent out to search and, with much difficulty, extreme delay and shell plating and belting damage, she was finally brought alongside in the harbour. *Isle of Thanet* was again damaged, this time on her

starboard quarter, in a 1938 collision with the quay at Folkestone on her arrival from Boulogne on 15th January.

The Southern Railway's normal practice of retaining one Strait of Dover steamer in reserve was abandoned in summer 1939 when its stand-by ship, *Isle of Thanet*, was moved to Southampton to provide daylight sailings on the increasingly popular St Malo service and, on 29th July, carried more than half of the 1,878 passengers embarking that day in three sailings to the Breton port.

On the Folkestone to Boulogne route, *Maid of Kent* made her last ever passenger sailing on 2nd September and on 21st May 1940 became a Second World War loss at Dieppe. The other two ships survived the war, with *Canterbury* restoring the 'Golden Arrow' service on 15th April 1946, carrying over 1,500 passengers on each of two inbound crossings that September, then opening a 26-mile Folkestone-Calais route on the first day of December. After sailings between Newhaven and Dieppe, *Isle of Thanet* (below) returned to the Folkestone service on 28th January 1947 and, when she developed propeller problems at Calais on 5th July 1948, *Canterbury* was called upon to make five Channel crossings in a day, to cater for the build-up of passengers.

Both ships later became associated with cross-Channel day excursions, thereby continuing a tradition in place since at least 1899 and particularly developed in 1923, when destinations from Kentish ports included not only Boulogne and Calais but also Dieppe. Their post-Second World War

popularity can be gauged from the events of 2nd August 1954 when *Isle of Thanet* embarked at Folkestone no fewer than 1,321 Boulogne day excursionists and *Canterbury* catered for the overflow of 350. Both steamers carried their fair share of the 339,000 passengers who used the route in summer 1963, hundreds of whom were delayed several hours on 4th August as a result of *Isle of Thanet* hitting the jetty at the French port. The conclusion of that summer season brought *Isle of Thanet*'s career to an end and she was followed out of service by *Canterbury* one year later, the latter vessel being seen departing for the breakers in August 1965. [*A.M.S. Russell collection; J. and M. Clarkson (2)*]

WORTHING 1928
Built for the Southern Railway by William Denny and Brothers Ltd., Dumbarton; 2,288gt, 297·7 feet
Six steam turbines single-reduction geared to two screw shafts by William Denny and Brothers Ltd., Dumbarton.

BRIGHTON 1933
Built for the Southern Railway by William Denny and Brothers Ltd., Dumbarton; 2,391gt, 298.1 feet
Six steam turbines single-reduction geared to two screw shafts by William Denny and Brothers Ltd., Dumbarton.

The town of Worthing was chosen, in preference to St Leonards, Chichester and Lewes, for the name of this new British ship and, in recognition of the majority French ownership of the Newhaven to Dieppe fleet, a Vicomtesse was chosen to perform the 1928 launching ceremony. With day and night passenger accommodation for 1,040 passengers, *Worthing* crossed from Dieppe on pre-service trials in 2 hours 37 minutes at an average slightly in excess of her contract speed of 24 knots. She entered passenger service on 5th September 1928, in time to make her contribution to the total of more than a quarter of a million passengers carried on the route that year.

The specification of the second ship – the name *Brighton* yet again being selected for a ship on the route – not only repeated the earlier requirement for a speed of 24 knots but also stipulated that this must be achievable in all weather conditions. She made her first visit to Dieppe with company guests on 7th April 1933, before entering normal service three days later. The centre photograph, showing *Brighton* at buoys in Dieppe harbour nearest the camera and *Worthing* alongside the quay, provides an opportunity to compare the appearance of the two vessels. The most obvious external differences are

the newer ship's extended bulwarks, steel-fronted wheelhouse and raised boat deck lifeboats. A squall of hurricane force threw *Worthing*'s starboard side heavily against the quay as she reached Newhaven on 25th February 1935. The following year, *Brighton*'s port propeller, tail shaft and hull bore the brunt of heavy contact with the foundations of the breakwater at Newhaven on a foggy 15th August: she again sustained damage on 15th April 1938, when she struck the pier at the entrance to Dieppe harbour.

Brighton completed her passenger service to Dieppe on 5th September 1939 and, as a Second

World War hospital carrier, ended her career at the port on 22nd May 1940, being sunk by a bomb explosion on the Greek ship *Galaxias* (4,398/1918), alongside which she was moored, as seen in the bottom photograph.

Worthing (pictured next page, top) survived the war but required an 11-month refit before resuming passenger service in March 1947. She was declared redundant at the end of 1954, the lack of a bow rudder precluding her regular use on other railway routes and resulting in her sale as a pilgrim carrier. [*A.M.S. Russell collection; Captain J.F. van Puyvelde; J. and M. Clarkson collection*]

TWICKENHAM FERRY and HAMPTON FERRY 1934, SHEPPERTON FERRY 1935

Built for the Southern Railway by Swan Hunter and Wigham Richardson Ltd., Newcastle-upon-Tyne; 2,839gt, 346·8 feet

Four steam turbines single-reduction geared to two screw shafts by Parsons Marine Steam Turbine Co. Ltd., Newcastle-upon-Tyne.

Following the 1929 introduction of the daytime 'Golden Arrow' between London and Paris, the Southern Railway decided to operate a sleeping car service between the two capital cities. By April 1933, tenders had been received from 15 shipyards for three identical coal-burning vessels for the Dover to Dunkerque sea connection, with Swan Hunter laying down the keels later that year. So that the water level could be adjusted to a constant height to counter a tidal variation of up to 25 feet, a special train ferry dock was needed at Dover: however, construction of this was massively delayed, because fissures in the chalk foundation were allowing water to come through the bottom at a faster rate than it could be pumped out. Work on the dock continued day and night but, even so, it was more than 18 months after the March 1935 delivery of the final ship, named *Shepperton Ferry*, that the first two ships commenced the planned train ferry service. In the early hours of 6th October 1936, *Hampton Ferry* crossed from Dover and *Twickenham Ferry* from

Dunkerque, the latter steamer having by then been transferred to the French flag, as a result of political pressure. In its first full year of operation, over 73,000 passengers travelled on the route, more than half using the through sleeping car service but the freight traffic carried on the daytime crossings was below expectations. On trials in bad weather, it was found that the vessels suffered from stability problems, so, to prolong the period of roll, 200 tons of old rails were cemented to the floor of their 25-car boat deck garages.

Unlike on other ships, where crane-handling of vehicles was the norm, motorists could drive on and off the train ferries and avail themselves of the passenger cabins, the number of which was in 1939 increased from eight

to fifteen. The last 'Night Ferry' London to Paris through service that year ran on 25th August, after which the British ships were requisitioned for Second World War mine laying duty. Whereas the pre-war arrangement was to use only two of the ships at any one time, planning for post-war services in 1944 included the summer employment of all three train ferries simultaneously, mainly to Boulogne, because of its shorter crossing time. The proposed daily sailing pattern called for one ship to carry the outbound 'Night Ferry' to Boulogne, return to Dover, then make a further round trip to Boulogne. A second vessel would convey the inbound 'Night Ferry' from Boulogne, then operate one Dover-Dunkerque-Dover voyage before returning to Boulogne. The third vessel would make a daytime round trip to Boulogne catering solely for motorists, whose cars would be stowed not only in the dedicated garage but also on the train deck, after the fitting of flush decking. The implementation of this plan would have required the provision of a specially dredged lay-by berth on the west side of the ferry dock at Dover, because of which this scheme was not adopted. However, Boulogne did later become the French terminal when the train ferries acted as temporary replacements for the dedicated car ferry ships. The 'Night Ferry' service between Dover and Dunkerque was restored on 16th December 1947 and the route became profitable in post-war years, in contrast to the loss it incurred between 1936 and 1939.

The top photograph on this page, taken at Dunkerque, shows the French *Twickenham Ferry*, ahead of *Shepperton Ferry,* which is also seen leaving Dover on a post war sailing (opposite page, middle). The stern loading area of *Hampton Ferry* is clear from the middle picture on this page: the two railway lines fan out to four on board the ship, with the twin funnels being placed athwartships between them and the garage being situated above the train deck. Seen again in the bottom photograph taken in 1962, *Hampton Ferry* was sold in 1969; *Shepperton Ferry* followed three years later, then *Twickenham Ferry*. [*J. and M. Clarkson; A.M.S. Russell collection; Ships in Focus; J. and M. Clarkson collection*]

INVICTA 1940

Built for the Southern Railway by William Denny and Brothers Ltd., Dumbarton Ltd.; 4,178gt, 336·5 feet
Four steam turbines single-reduction geared to two screw shafts by William Denny and Brothers Ltd., Dumbarton.

Early in 1939, a coal-burning vessel was sought by the SR as a replacement for its 1915 *Biarritz* on the Strait of Dover services. Competitive tenders were submitted by John Brown, J. Samuel White, Thornycroft, Swan Hunter, Barclay Curle, Fairfield, Cammell Laird and Denny, whose prices ranged from £290,500 to £332,000 and delivery between 15 and 20 months. Denny won on price and delivery and, in June 1939, the name *Invicta* was approved for the new vessel, as was the inclusion of a stabiliser, which, if not successful, would be removed without financial obligation. As in the case of *Biarritz*, early plans for the ship were thrown into disarray by the outbreak of war and it was not until 15th October 1946, after post-war refit and conversion to oil-burning, that *Invicta* first saw commercial cross-Channel service and not until autumn

1949 that the planned stabilisers were finally installed. The photograph above shows the ship awaiting her maiden voyage while, in the middle picture, the vessel is seen leaving Calais, after the removal of her bridge wing cabs and the replacement of her original radar

equipment. Her fine lines are shown to good effect in the bottom photograph.

To counter the threat of airline competition, the Southern Railway considered a 1944 proposal to introduce two smaller but faster vessels for the Dover to Calais route, designed to carry a train load of about 300 passengers at a speed of at least 40 knots – nearly twice that of *Invicta*. A shaft-horse-power of 35,000, as opposed to the 11,000 of *Invicta*, would reduce the Dover to Calais crossing time by half an hour to a mere 45 minutes and cut the London to Paris city centre-to-city centre journey time by at least that. With a length of only 240 feet, compared with the 336 of *Invicta,* there would be no need for cabins or full restaurant facilities but one of the factors causing its rejection was that rough seas, which usually occur in the Strait of Dover about 74 days a year, would not only make the crossing uncomfortable for passengers but possibly also delay their arrival.

Invicta was the usual Dover to Calais link for the luxury 'Golden Arrow' service and the ship carried an average of 51,000 passengers each August during her first three summers. She rarely deviated from that route, although an exception occurred on 6th September 1958 when adverse conditions caused all Calais and Boulogne passengers to be diverted to Newhaven, instead of Dover or Folkestone, with the result that *Invicta* arrived at the Sussex port from Calais, then departed that same day for Boulogne. An extra passenger deck resulted in *Invicta*'s gross tonnage being more than 40% greater than any other vessel in the SR fleet in 1946 and she remained the largest railway vessel on the cross-Channel routes to France until the end of her service in 1972. *[Author's collection; A.M.S. Russell collection; J. and M. Clarkson]*

LONDRES 1943 and ARROMANCHES 1947

Built for Société Nationale des Chemins de Fer by Forges et Chantiers de la Mediterranee, Le Havre; 2,404gt, 310 feet (Londres), 299·3 feet (Arromanches)
Two steam turbines single-reduction geared by Forges et Chantiers de la Mediterranee, La Seyne.

Approved in January 1939 as replacements for the elderly French steamers on the Dieppe to Newhaven route, construction of these two vessels became engulfed by the Second World War. Captured on the slipway at Le Havre in June 1940, the first ship was completed for the German Navy in 1943 and it was not until November 1945 that *Londres* made her first visit to Dieppe. This was followed by a courtesy call at Newhaven the following month, prior to her post-war refit, which was prolonged by an outbreak of fire on 4th February 1947. With work finally completed, the ship achieved a speed of 24·41 knots on trials between Le Havre and Dieppe in early April that year and entered service to Newhaven on the 18th.

Her sister, ordered at the same time as *Londres* but not completed until after the war, was named *Arromanches* and made her first crossing from Dieppe to Newhaven on 16th August 1947. Both the French vessels were fitted with a new type of davit which permitted the lifeboats to be raised six feet above boat deck level, when sea conditions permitted, thereby increasing deck space for passengers. In the upper photograph, *Arromanches*, nearest the camera, has her three after boats on each side so raised while, in the distance, *Londres* has at least one similarly stowed.

The turn of the year 1948 to 1949 brought strong south-westerly gales and heavy seas in the English Channel. On 30th December, 312 passengers from Dieppe found that their rough passage did not end on arrival off the English south coast because, after three failed attempts to enter Newhaven harbour, *Arromanches* had to shelter outside for five hours. Conditions were even worse on her 1st January sailing from Dieppe, with the result that 109 passengers were forced to endure three Channel crossings in high seas before their ship could finally enter Newhaven. In 1953 and 1954, 90% of passengers on the route travelled third-class.

The 1954 withdrawal of *Worthing* distorted the even balance between British and French registered ships on the Newhaven-Dieppe route, so, to correct this, *Londres* underwent the third nationality change of her short career, re-entering service from Newhaven to Dieppe under the Red Ensign on 27th May 1955, after a six-month refit in South Wales. Official documents listed the ship's maximum speed at that time as 24·95 knots, giving a fuel oil consumption of 7·31 tons per hour, in sharp contrast to the 2·1 tons at her economical speed of 15·2 knots.

Londres ended her railway service on 6th October 1963, in preparation for the 1964 inauguration of car ferry sailings on the route. *Arromanches* (below in June 1963) continued in service and left Dieppe on 8th July 1964 with 677 passengers, mostly French schoolchildren, when the combination of a south-westerly gale and a low tide resulted in her going aground on arrival off Newhaven. After drifting eastwards in Seaford Bay, she remained stuck for nearly three hours, in what proved to be her final season in cross-Channel service. *[A.M.S. Russell collection; J. and M. Clarkson]*

FALAISE 1947

Built for the Southern Railway by William Denny and Brothers Ltd., Dumbarton; 3,710gt, 299·8 feet
Steam turbines single-reduction geared to two screw shafts by William Denny and Brothers Ltd., Dumbarton.

In April 1940, the Southern Railway obtained a quotation of £252,000 from Denny for the construction of a new steamer, 60% larger in gross tonnage but slightly shorter in length than the 1924 sisters *Dinard* and *St Briac*, so as to be suitable for all its day and night Southampton services. The intervention of the Second World War delayed the start of work until February 1946 and, bearing the name *Falaise*, she was completed the following year, the cost having by then increased to £560,260. The vessel set out on her maiden voyage from Southampton to St Malo on 14th July 1947 and carried over 12,000 passengers on her twice-weekly round voyages on the route that season, before being transferred to Dover for two and a half weeks on the 'Golden Arrow' service to Calais.

She was the first merchant ship to be delivered already fitted with Denny-Brown stabilisers, the device first installed in the company's Channel Islands' steamer *Isle of Sark* (2,211/1932) but now improved by the addition of tail flaps to the fins. Such was still the experimental nature of the *Falaise* installation that the £10,000 cost was not included in the ship's purchase price and payment was made only after 90-minute trials during the passage from Dover to Southampton had confirmed the equipment to be operationally successful.

In 1948, she re-introduced short cross-Channel cruises, first started by *St Briac*, and over the years these took her also to the French ports of Boulogne, Cherbourg, Dieppe, Le Havre and Rouen. After one of her 94 cruises *Falaise* became the centre of attention in 1951, when it was revealed that the senior British diplomats Burgess and Maclean had defected to Russia during a St Malo cruise call.

Until that year, war damage at the port resulted in *Falaise* anchoring in the River Rance, off St Malo, and the top photograph records the ship's first alongside berthing in the enclosed basin, which became her destination each summer until 29th September 1963.

It is relevant to note that, in February 1945, the Southern Railway's five-year shipbuilding plan included the 1949 ordering of a new 2,500 gross ton Newhaven-Dieppe car ferry. In reality, it took until 1964 for the car ferry plan to materialise and, when it did, it was not with the use of a new build but with the

conversion of *Falaise*. With her gross tonnage reduced to 2,416, the middle photograph shows the ship arriving at Dieppe in 1964 in her new guise, following the inauguration of car ferry services on 1st June. Such was the popularity of the new service that over 23,000 vehicles had been carried by mid-September that first year.

As a result of a number of collisions with the piers, her 1967 annual overhaul at Middlesbrough was the third

successive year that a replacement bow rudder was fitted. In her second year of car ferry service, the white paintwork was stepped down one deck from beneath the bridge to the stern, as can be seen from the bottom view depicting the steamer leaving Dieppe, after the 1968 addition of the Newhaven to Dieppe joint service flag to the buff-painted section of her funnel. Although overshadowed by the arrival of new French purpose-built vessels, *Falaise*

had completed more than 4,300 car ferry crossings by the date of her withdrawal from Newhaven at the end of the 1972 season. Despite discussions regarding her transfer to the French or even Finnish flag, it was decided that she would be retained under the Red Ensign to inaugurate railway car ferry services between Weymouth and the Channel Islands the following year. *[Author's collection]*

NORMANNIA 1952
Built for the British Transport Commission by William Denny and Brothers Ltd., Dumbarton; 3,543gt, 309 feet
Two double-reduction geared steam turbines by William Denny and Brothers Ltd., Dumbarton

The desirability of ordering what proved to be the final new passenger ship for railway steamer services from Southampton began as early as December 1944, with 1949 set by the Southern Railway as the year for the placing of such an order. This plan was based on a 77% increase in 1938 passenger carryings on the St Malo summer service, compared with the previous year, and the assumption that two ships would be required if the route's popularity continued in post-war years. These St Malo passenger figures were in marked contrast to those on the route to Le Havre, which had declined by 40% between 1928 and 1938. With cargo traffic on the Le Havre route down by a massive 75% during the same period, the Southern Railway proposed to arrest the decline by the introduction of train ferry vessels similar to, but more powerful than, those operating from Dover (see *Twickenham Ferry* above), with a view to performing twice daily sailings either on the 83-mile Southampton to Cherbourg crossing or, more particularly, on the 106-mile route to Le Havre, where the enclosed dock system would lend itself to the construction of a terminal of relatively

simple design. This service would cater not only for passengers and vehicles but also for port-to-port cargo and through rail freight. Implementing this project called for the ordering of two 3,000 gross ton train ferries but post-war finances, after the nationalisation of the railways in 1948, were such that no order was forthcoming. Consequently, the new Southampton passenger vessel, finally launched in 1951, did not join *Falaise* in augmenting the St Malo sailings, as originally proposed, but acted as replacement for the 1912 *Hantonia* on the service to Le Havre.

Reviving the name of *Hantonia*'s sister, which had become a war loss, the new *Normannia* entered service on 3rd March 1952, after successfully completing the trials she is seen undertaking in the top photograph. In a comparison between the old and new steamers, it was noted that the weight of the geared turbine machinery and Scotch boilers in the 1912 ship, which developed 5,000 shaft-horse-power, was twice that of the new vessel's water-tube boilers and 8,000 shaft-horse-power geared turbines and that, in the old vessel, the total length of the machinery and boiler space was approximately 30% greater than in the 1952 ship. *Normannia*'s first year of service was marred by a collision, the results of which are clearly visible in the right hand picture. In thick fog on 26th December, her bow struck the Union-Castle liner *Arundel Castle* (19,216/1921) which was alongside her Itchen River berth. It was 44 days before *Normannia* could resume service.

Her Southampton-based sailings came to an end on 4th December 1963, after which she was sent for conversion to a 2,219 gross ton stern-loading car ferry for Dover service and this transformation is revealed in the top photograph on the following page, taken after the addition of the railway emblem on her, by then, red and black-painted funnel. Her inaugural car ferry

crossing to Boulogne took place on 20th April 1964 and, with accommodation for 111 cars and 500 passengers, it was primarily with this route that she would be associated over the following years. Primarily, but certainly not exclusively, as all too frequently she was switched to other services, often as temporary replacement vessel, with her new French destinations including Calais, Cherbourg, Dieppe, Dunkerque and St Malo. She was involved in a number of unusual incidents and events, such as when a container of fish fell off its lorry on to other vehicles in rough seas on 12th November 1969; when a fatal accident occurred on her car deck the following 5th August; when she undertook over 250 round trips under the French flag during summer 1973 and when a submerged section of concrete in Dover harbour ripped a 10-foot hole in her hull on 18th July 1974, causing the flooding of her engine room and car deck. *Normannia*'s cross-Channel service ended on 6th May 1978, following which she was sold for breaking up. *[Author's collection; Fotoflite incorporating Skyfotos]*

LORD WARDEN 1952

Built for the British Transport Commission by William Denny and Brothers Ltd., Dumbarton; 3,333gt, 361 feet
Two direct-reduction geared steam turbines by William Denny and Brothers Ltd., Dumbarton.

Approval was granted in December 1949 for the construction of the first specially-designed stern-loading car ferry for Strait of Dover service. In the selection of names, a return was made to the early 1900s with the preferred choice of *Onward* but, as this was not available, *Lord Warden* was adopted in its place. The new ship, seen at Southampton in the centre photograph on 18th May 1952 prior to her maiden voyage, made her first call at Boulogne on 14th June 1952, on passage from Southampton to Dover and, during the course of her first voyage from the Kentish port two days later, her master took the opportunity of exchanging messages with the current Lord Warden of the Cinque Ports, Winston Churchill.

The ship's introduction into service was timed to coincide with completion of Boulogne's new maritime station and car ferry terminal, thereby putting an end to crane handling at the French port but not, for one further year, at Dover. With a capacity for 120 cars, *Lord Warden* carried more than 16,000 cars, 500 coaches and 2,000 motor cycles in her initial five months' service and the bottom photograph shows the ship approaching the Boulogne ramp on one of her early sailings. The following year, the ship embarked over

100 cars for a special Dover-Boulogne crossing on 21st January: they were participants in the Monte Carlo Rally which had started out from Glasgow. On the 10th of the following month and less than two weeks after the stern-loading Denny-built car ferry *Princess Victoria* (2,694/1947) sank in a gale whilst crossing from Scotland to Northern Ireland, the securing stays on *Lord Warden*'s folding stern doors snapped as the vessel dipped in a

huge wave during a Channel gale. In her case, very little water was shipped and the doors could immediately be shored up and later strengthened.

The improved terminal facilities and *Lord Warden*'s introduction contributed to a massive boost in the total of vehicles carried on the Boulogne route from 82,000 in 1951 to 216,000 in 1954. During that latter year, the vessel made history on 26th September, when a

BBC mobile transmitter van, with a 110-foot aerial, was used for the first-ever television transmission from a moving ship at sea, as the steamer headed for Boulogne in lively conditions. Two years later, *Lord Warden* was involved in a collision in patchy thick fog on 7th July 1956, sustaining extensive damage to her bows, anchors and bow rudder as a result of ramming the French motor vessel *Tamba* (5,100/1954) three miles west of Cap Gris Nez.

A problem with funnel fumes was tackled by experimentally raising the exhaust outlets, as shown in the top photograph, prior to the final solution, seen on 22nd August 1976 (above), in the form of the addition of a 'fireman's helmet'. After a career of 27 years, *Lord Warden*'s cross-Channel service came to an end with her sale in 1979. *[J. and M. Clarkson; Author's collection (2); J. and M. Clarkson]*

PUTTING THE RECORD STRAIGHT

Letters, additions, amendments and photographs relating to features in any issues of 'Record' are welcomed. Letters may be lightly edited. Note that comments on multi-part articles are consolidated and included in the issue of 'Record' following the final part. Senders of e-mails are asked to include their postal address.

Scottish coaster corrections

I've just read through Graeme Somner's article on Scottish steam coasters, wherein he mentions that *Wisbech* was built as *JWN* 'during 1916 in Yorkshire'. That sounded a bit vague and on checking not quite geographically correct, as she was built by Warren at New Holland on the Lincolnshire

side of the Humber. Her first owner was William Nettleton of Hull. In 1930 she became *St. Kevin* of Stanley Harding before becoming *Wisbech* in 1932.
GEORGE ROBINSON, Southwood Cottage, Southwood Road, Cottingham, East Yorkshire HU16 5AJ

It was again for a couple of days very quiet (says my wife) after the arrival of 'Record' 48. One small correction if I may: on page 253 *Dunmoir* arrived in Ghent on 19th July 1954 to be broken up by the local scrap yard of Van Heyghen Freres.
FLORENT VAN OTTERDYK, Antwerpsesteenweg 40, B-2720 Zwijndrecht (Burcht), Belgium.

GRAND UNION (SHIPPING) LTD.
Roy Fenton and Alan Faulkner

The Grand Union (Shipping) Ltd. was unique. Shipping companies have often been founded by merchants, brokers, master mariners, railway companies and by industrialists, but Grand Union is the only known British shipping line formed by a canal company.[1]

The line's parent, the Grand Union Canal Co. Ltd.,[2] came into being on 1st January 1929 as a merger of five canal companies.[3] This meant canal routes from Birmingham and Leicester to London were at last under common ownership, with outlets to the Thames at both Brentford and Limehouse. In 1932 the company also took over three further navigations, taking its line into Nottinghamshire.[4]

The new company's founders were well aware that it would require dynamic leadership to reverse the trend of falling traffic on British canals, and the company went on to promote and actively publicise the Grand Union and the services it could provide.[5] An experimental pair of narrow boats which could take an increased payload had already been ordered and were launched in February 1929. Soon afterwards a small canal carrying company was bought, Associated Canal Carriers Ltd. of Northampton, and its fleet augmented by six further pairs of narrow boats built to the new design.

In March 1934 the carrying company was renamed the Grand Union Canal Carrying Co. Ltd. (GUCCC) and its capital increased to £20,000, enabling a further six pairs of narrow boats to be ordered. Larger orders followed in January 1935 with 24 pairs ordered from Harland and Wolff Ltd. at Woolwich and 12 from W.J. Yarwood and Sons Ltd. at Northwich. In both cases these ship builders and repairers were grateful recipients of orders which kept their yards occupied during a serious depression in ship building. Eventually, they and other builders delivered a remarkable total of 186 pairs of narrow boats to GUCCC.

The Grand Union also improved its waterways, and aided by a Government guaranteed loan it replaced

Four Grand Union narrow boats nearing completion in W.J. Yarwood's yard at Northwich, Cheshire. They are *Rufford, Renfrew, Renton* and *Reading*. All were delivered to Grand Union in October 1936. *[Collection of the late Clive Guthrie]*

52 seven-foot wide locks with 51 14-foot locks and replaced bridges, enabling much larger boats to traverse the canal route on its line through Warwick up to Birmingham. Here, and on the former Grand Junction Canal between Brentford and Braunston, there was also much bank protection and dredging work.

Grand Union Shipping
To find traffic for its carrying company, the Grand Union decided to exploit its facilities at Limehouse, the Regent's Canal Dock. This 11-acre dock could take ships up to 350-feet in length and 60 feet wide, and had a depth over sills of 28-feet at Trinity high water mark.[6] Already using the dock were regular steamers serving Bergen, Bremen, Hamburg, Koln and other Rhine ports, Dutch and Spanish ports. Whilst these services provided some traffic for the canal, the company was anxious to build this up. There was an important development on 14th October 1935 when the steamer *Dona Isabel* (784/1924) entered the dock and discharged 1,250 tons of imported iron and steel from the Continent into two dozen pairs of narrow boats for delivery to Birmingham and the South Staffordshire area. This put the GUCCC into dispute with the railways who claimed it breached

existing agreements, but the company held its nerve and iron and steel traffic became regular. So much so that in February 1936 John Miller (Shipping) Ltd. was appointed the GUCCC's agents for the traffic from France, Belgium and the Netherlands for an initial three-year period.

In October John Miller himself was appointed a director of both the GUCCC and the parent Grand Union Canal Company. A further development at Regent's Canal Dock was the formation of the Grand Union (Stevedoring and Wharfage) Co. Ltd. in May 1937 to bring much of the ship-working and wharfage at the dock under the Grand Union's direct control.

It was almost certainly at John Miller's suggestion that on 18th August 1937 the stevedoring company acquired the Dutch-built steamer *Merwede* for £8,000.[7] She was hired at £140 per quarter to the GUCCC and renamed *Marsworth* to begin a regular service to Rotterdam and Antwerp.[8] Early in September the company time chartered the Dutch motor coaster *Brinda* (200/1936) for a month at £210 per 15 days and the steamer *Alfa* for four months at £350 per month.[9] C.C. Sheaff was appointed to manage the new shipping department.

In this aerial view of Regent's Canal Dock in 1928 several ships can be seen, amidst a chaos of lighters and a few canal craft. A collier is at the mechanised jetty of the Regent's Discharging Co. Ltd. in the north east corner of the Dock. This jetty was completed in 1926, and its main employment was discharging coal to be shipped by canal craft to the Kensal Green Works of the Gas, Light and Coal Company.

The Dock's ship lock entrance from the Thames can be seen to the south. The entrance to the Regent's Canal is beneath one of the railway arches to the north (this railway is now part of the Docklands Light Railway). Beyond the Dock to the east is the Limehouse Cut which, remarkably, was not connected to the Dock until after it closed to commercial shipping.

Although reasonably busy during the early 1960s, by 1968 an average of just two ships per week were using Regent's Canal Dock, and its then owners, British Waterways, announced that it would close to shipping in May 1969. As part of the London Docklands development, Limehouse Basin as it is now called, serves pleasure craft and is surrounded by housing rather than by warehouses and cranes. *[Alan Faulkner collection]*

Alongside Bergen Wharf in Regent's Canal Dock in 1938 a pair of Grand Union Carrying Co. Ltd. narrow boats are pinned against the side of the Dutch motor coaster *Kemphaan* (343/1936) by Thames lighters. The size of the latter emphasises the small scale of narrow boats. *[British Waterways Archive /Alan Faulkner collection]*

No photographs have been found of Grand Union ships in the Regent's Canal Dock, but this delightful view in the 1950s shows cargo being transhipped between British Waterways' narrow boats and the British motor coaster *Milborne* (332/1941). The other three ships visible are all owned by General Steam, from the left the motor vessel *Whitewing* (1,102/1953), the steamer *Groningen* (1,205/1928) and either the *Ptarmigan* or *Woodcock* (959/1948). *[British Waterways Archive/Alan Faulkner collection]*

Chartered by Grand Union in 1937, the tiny Dutch motor coaster *Brinda* was photographed on the Thames on 26th September 1953, flying what looks suspiciously like the DFDS houseflag. *[Len Sawyer/Roy Fenton collection]*

It was soon decided to set up a subsidiary company to handle the shipping activities and Grand Union (Shipping) Ltd. was incorporated on 27th November 1937 with an initial share capital of £5,000. John Miller was appointed Chairman at the first board meeting in December. The new company took over the Grand Union (Stevedoring and Wharfage) Co. Ltd. for £7.500, and early in 1938 acquired the assets of the Shipping Department of the Grand Union Canal Carrying Co. Ltd.[10] The shipping company traded as the Regent's Line.

There was a proposal to co-operate with companies running services on the River Rhine between Basle, Strasbourg and Antwerp, transhipping their cargoes at the Belgian port, but it was decided that initially the company would concentrate on the iron and steel business from Antwerp.[11] A service to Rotterdam was added in the autumn of 1938, cargoes including imports of Dutch vegetables, and from January 1939 this required two ships. At the same time there was also a proposal to discuss a joint service to Ghent with the General Steam Navigation Company, although this was later deferred. In its first year the new company was anticipated to make a £3,000 loss but in fact it soon became profitable and in two years brought 57,592 tons of freight into Regent's Canal Dock of which 12,152 went on up the canal. There was also some export traffic.

In August 1938 negotiations began with Anthony Veder N.V. of Rotterdam which resulted in the company being appointed as general agents in both the United Kingdom and (through an associated company) Belgium for a new service from Europe to the Great Lakes. In return the Grand Union appointed the Veder company as its general agents in the Netherlands. The new service was to start early in 1939 and, whilst it was expected to operate at a loss for 18 months, this loss would be more than offset by income from the Veder agency. During the period the Great Lakes were normally frozen, from October to March, the ships on the Canadian service were to operate from Palestine and Spain with fruit. Veder agreed to give Grand Union the agency for these ships, to consign the traffic to Regent's Canal Dock wherever possible and to try and induce other members of the Fruit Pool to do likewise.

The resulting Oranje Line began a regular fortnightly service between London and St John's in Newfoundland, Montreal, Toronto, Hamilton, Cleveland, Detroit, Milwaukee and Chicago using four modern, Norwegian-built steamships: *Prins Frederik Hendrik* (1,288/1936), *Prins Maurits* (1,287/1936), *Prins Willem Van Oranje* (1,303/1938) and *Prins Willem II* (1,304/1939) to which was later added the Dutch-built motor ship *Prins Willem III* (1,524/1939). During winter, calls were restricted to the eastern Canadian ports.

Grand Union at war

The outbreak of the Second World War caused major disruption to trading patterns, and both Antwerp and Rotterdam services were suspended on 4th September. The Antwerp service, but not that to Rotterdam, was re-opened in December. Despite this reduction in services, the company offered £9,250 in December 1939 for the steamer *Kathleen*, an offer which was accepted and the steamer was renamed *Blisworth*. Unlike *Marsworth*, she was fitted with degaussing equipment. Both the company's ships were armed with Lewis guns.

Although its regular services came to a complete halt in mid-1940, the company's ships could find plenty of profitable work in the wartime tramp and charter markets. Their profitability would be reduced somewhat when, along with most British ships, they were requisitioned by the Ministry of Shipping and its successor the Ministry of War Transport. *Blisworth* was the first, taken on time charter at £1,107 per month on 23rd September 1940, with *Marsworth* following on 1st October. With the Netherlands overrun, the five Veder ships were also time chartered to the Ministry, Grand Union receiving a modest 1% of the hire charge, presumably for agency work. Three of these ships were to be lost: *Prins Frederik Hendrik* bombed and sunk by aircraft on 8th March 1941,

Prins Willem van Oranje (1,303/1938) survived the war and after one German and two Indian owners was scrapped at Bombay in 1966. *[World Ship Society Ltd.]*

The Belfast-owned steamer *Kathleen* (above) was bought in December 1939 and renamed *Blisworth* (1) shortly before wartime regulations forbad name changes. Despite being 48 years old, she could still find a buyer when Grand Union finished with her in 1950, and as *Holdernidd* (below) she gave six further years' service to Hull's Holderness Steamship Co. Ltd. She appears to be in excellent condition, the only change since she was photographed as *Kathleen* is the fitting of a wheel house. *[Ships in Focus; Fotoflite incorporating Skyfotos]*

Prins Willem II torpedoed and sunk by a submarine on 8th April 1941, and Prins Willem III also sunk by aircraft, on 27th March 1943.

Germany was not the only enemy Grand Union faced. In February 1939 the Attorney General, acting on behalf of several shipping companies, started proceedings against the canal, stevedoring and shipping companies, claiming they had no powers to operate shipping. The outbreak of war caused the case to be deferred, but the threat of legal action led to an all-embracing Act of Parliament being passed in July 1943, in the face of opposition from the Chamber of Shipping, General Steam and other shipping companies, giving Grand Union powers to carry by land, sea, water or air. As a result Grand Union (Shipping) Ltd., previously a subsidiary of the stevedoring company, now became a wholly-owned subsidiary of the parent canal company.

In February 1944 the company acquired its third steamer, the *Eskwood*, the capital having just been increased to £75,000 which more than covered her purchase price of a modest £17,000. When wartime regulations were relaxed in 1946, *Eskwood* was to be renamed *Kilworth*, continuing the established practice of naming the ships after locations on the canal.

Board minutes for May 1944 coyly record *Blisworth* and *Marsworth* as being 'on special service'. In fact, *Marsworth* was loading at Cardiff in preparation for Operation Neptune and on 12th June she sailed from the Solent for Omaha Beach. She then shuttled between the Solent and Normandy until August. *Eskwood* was also involved, sailing from the Thames on June 5th to proceed, again via the Solent, for the Eastern Task Force area. After six further voyages to the beaches, *Eskwood* was damaged on 14th August when a heavy swell lifted her and the steamer *Westburn* (2,842/1929) causing their sterns to come into contact, with considerable damage to *Eskwood's* stern and steering gear. This effectively ended her participation, as she was towed back to Southampton, arriving on 24th August.[12] *Blisworth* is recorded in January 1945 as visiting Antwerp once again; the port had been reopened to Allied shipping in late November 1944.

On 19th November 1944 the company was allowed to order a new motor vessel from the Burntisland Shipbuilding Co. Ltd. for £57,090.[13]

Eskwood (above), bought in 1944, was renamed Kilworth in 1946. [Bristol Series/J. and M. Clarkson]

Two new ships were delivered to Grand Union from Burntisland immediately after the Second World War. Increasingly, these ventured into the coastal tramp trades and Knebworth (right) is arriving at Preston, a long way from her Regent's Canal Dock base, on 31st July 1950 with china clay from Fowey. The second vessel delivered to the company from Burntisland was Bosworth (below). [Douglas Cochrane/ World Ship Society Ltd.; Ships in Focus]

A second order for an identical ship at the same price followed in March 1945. The first, the *Knebworth*, was launched on 16th February 1946 and was completed in June 1946. Her sister ship, *Bosworth*, was launched two days after *Knebworth* but was not completed until September when she brought the fleet up to five.

The Second World War, which eventually meant the suspension of all trade to northern Europe, and the diversion of traffic away from London, meant a decline in traffic through Regent's Canal Dock, the 722,467 tons handled in 1938 being reduced to 359,797 tons in 1940, although it thereafter slowly climbed towards its prewar levels. This was helped by the comprehensive dredging of the Dock by the Tilbury Contracting and Dredging Co. Ltd. in the summer of 1944, costing nearly £31,700 and which restored the Dock to its full working depth of 20-feet.

Post-war expansion

With the war over and two new ships available, ambitious plans were laid to continue and develop services. The company was independent of freight conferences, meaning it could set its own rates, undercutting other operators if it so wished. The Antwerp and Rotterdam services were resumed jointly with Walford Lines Ltd. and, probably because of this, only *Marsworth* was assigned to these, running to Antwerp. An important traffic was in copper via Antwerp; other cargoes included wool and tallow which were trans-shipped in Regent's Canal Dock into lighters for delivery to Thames-side premises or landed for warehouse storage. The company also used Samuel Williams' wharf at Dagenham. A service from London to Copenhagen was proposed in March 1946, and one to Oslo early in 1947, with the *Knebworth* and later *Bosworth* being allocated to these routes. In late 1947 there was also discussion about opening services to Gothenburg and, jointly, to Finland, although there is no evidence that the latter ever started.

There was work beyond liner services, and increasingly the Grand Union ships were to move into tramping. In late 1947 and 1948 the company was carrying scrap from Hamburg (where there was a plentiful supply) to English east coast ports in conjunction with the ships of George Tom and Co. Ltd.[14] From May 1948

to January 1949, the company held a contract with the Board of Trade to ship wood pulp from Norway to the Thames, Ridham Dock, Rochester, Grimsby or Bristol. Another contract with the same customer in the spring of 1948 involved loading timber for the UK at Hamburg or Bremen.

This additional work was beyond the capacity of the fleet, even at its largest extent of five vessels. The company considered selling some of its ageing steamers in favour of new motor ships but, probably because of impending nationalisation (see below), preferred chartering. Steamers time chartered included the *Master Nicolas* (811/1908) for 12 months from April 1947 and Monroe's *Kylebay* (787/1911) for 12 months from May 1947. The motor ship *Springcrag* (322/1941) was chartered for the services to Copenhagen and Stockholm.

Nationalisation and sale

Soon after the war it became obvious that the Grand Union Canal Company together with its canal carrying and shipping subsidiaries would be nationalised to become part of the British Transport Commission. In November 1947 George A. Tom and Co. Ltd. offered to purchase all the shipping company's 40,000 shares at £3 per share and to repay a £35,000 loan made by the stevedoring company towards the purchase price of the two new ships. The potential owners agreed they would continue the existing services into Regent's Canal Dock and retain the staff, but the directors would be required to resign.

By this time negotiations for the nationalisation of the Grand Union, along with most other canal and railway companies, were well advanced, the enabling Transport Bill having received the Royal Assent on 6th August 1947. Whilst the directors were willing to accept the terms offered by Tom after settling a disagreement about the payment of a dividend, approval would have been needed from the Ministry of Transport. This could not be obtained before vesting day on 1st January 1948 and the final decision had to be deferred to the British Transport Commission.

In the event the sale of 75% of the shipping company's shares went ahead in the late summer of 1948, but to the General Steam Navigation Co. Ltd. who, ironically, had earlier been one of the concerns contesting the Grand Union's powers to operate shipping. No doubt the company was pleased to take over a concern that had been a thorn in its side. The Grand Union (Shipping) Ltd. continued to trade under the same name, and still had its own board of directors, including George A. Tom and N.W. Spratt who were ship owners in their own right and in the former's case retained a substantial shareholding.

As an aside, it is interesting to speculate why the sale went ahead following nationalisation at the beginning of 1948, as new negotiations were clearly instigated with General Steam, who presumably made a better offer than George Tom. Although the Docks and Inland Waterways Executive did not operate ships itself, its sister organisation within the British Transport Commission - the Railway

Monroe Brothers' steamer *Kylebay* was chartered for 12 months in May 1947. She had been built at Middlesbrough in 1911 as *Hampshire Coast* for a predecessor of Coast Lines Ltd., and was bought by Monroes in 1936. *[J.F. van Puyvelde]*

Executive - took over and continued to run a large fleet of ships inherited from its four railway company predecessors. The Labour Government's policy was very much in favour of nationalisation of transport, so it is surprising that Grand Union (Shipping) Ltd. was sold to the private sector rather than be incorporated within the railway fleet.

A new regime

Gradually, Grand Union (Shipping) Ltd. began to feel the influence of its new owner, who did not have the same incentive to serve Regent's Canal Dock as did the canal company. First casualties were the Copenhagen and Oslo services, ceasing during July 1949: no doubt they were competing with those of General Steam. Ships were sold and not always replaced: early that year *Marsworth*, the company's first ship, had been sold to Indian owners, and in 1950 the *Blisworth* (1) went to Hull owners and the *Kilworth* to George A. Tom and Co. Ltd. The only replacement was the Bristol-built motor ship *Somersetbrook* purchased in July 1949 and renamed *Marsworth* (2). These were not the only departures: George Tom and N.W. Spratt left the board in January 1950, the former selling his 4,000 shares to General Steam as part of the process of the latter company assuming full control.

In May 1950 an anticipated loss for the year persuaded the directors to approach Walford Lines to discuss terminating their joint service, and *Marsworth* began to serve both Antwerp and Rotterdam, making one sailing each week. She proved too large for the cargo offering, however, and in 1951 was sent tramping whilst her place was taken by the chartered *Polly M* (380/1937). Efforts to find remunerative work for the fleet saw *Bosworth* being offered to Macandrews for their Spanish fruit trade. They initially agreed to take her for just one voyage as a trial, but this proved successful so for several months she ran for them between Spain, UK, Antwerp and Rotterdam. By October 1952 she was working between Liverpool and Bordeaux for Moss Hutchison, a subsidiary of P&O, along with General Steam. In late 1951 *Knebworth* was fitted for foreign voyages, this apparently requiring only that she carry a motor lifeboat, in order that she could be chartered to Moss Hutchison and to General Steam for their Hamburg service.

Grand Union's post-war policy of advertising the use of British ships led them to charter several small motor ships from Metcalf Motor Coasters Ltd., whereas they might have preferred cheaper Dutch coasters. The Dutch-built *Polly M* of 1937 (above) was chartered in 1951 for services to Antwerp. In the 1950s the company chartered the *Rose-Julie M* (below) which had been built at Hessle in 1941 as *Empire Bank* and bought by Metcalf in 1945. [Both: Ships in Focus]

Small financial losses continued, prompting a proposal to use chartered Dutch motor coasters following the loss of *Marsworth* (2) in November 1953. This idea foundered when it was pointed out that the company advertised itself as running only British ships, and hence the *Brier Rose* was acquired and given the same name as the ship she replaced. Two motor coasters were taken on charter, the British-flagged *Rose Julie M* (402/1941) and *Walcrag* (322/1941) (the latter the former *Springcrag*, now owned by Walfords who, despite earlier intentions, continued the joint service to Rotterdam for several years).

In 1955 there were several proposals to buy ships, including an unspecified tanker and the motor ship *Yarmouth Trader* (945/1946). The latter's owner was the Great Yarmouth Shipping Co. Ltd. which had been bought by General Steam in 1946 and which shared chairman I.M. Hooper with Grand Union. As an economy measure, the two companies had also shared a marine superintendent since 1952. The next proposal was to buy the new German coaster *Max Sieghold* (956/1956), but this did not prove feasible. Instead, in August 1956 five UK yards were asked to tender for a new motor ship. Although the board minutes indicate that the order was to go to Burntisland, which had built the company's only other new buildings, the *Blisworth* (2) was delivered by A. Hall and Co. Ltd., Aberdeen in November 1957, bringing the fleet back to four.

The agency work for Anthony Veder's Oranje Line came to an end

The motor coaster *Springcrag* (above) was chartered by Grand Union twice, once whilst owned by Springwell Shipping Co. Ltd., London and again in 1954 when owned by Walford Lines Ltd., London as *Walcrag* (below). She had been built at Faversham in 1941 as *Empire Crag*. The photograph of *Springcrag* above was taken in July 1951, and shows that she was an early victim of the trend to reduce cargo gear, as no derricks are visible. By the 1970s when she had become *Spithead Trader* (her fifth name under the British flag), her masts had been reduced to mere poles for carrying navigation lights. She finally became a crane ship, and was still listed by 'Lloyd's Register' in 2000. *[Tom Rayner/J. and M. Clarkson; Ships in Focus]*

Blisworth of 1957 in General Steam Navigation colours, October 1965. *[Ships in Focus]*

in 1956, and the remaining liner services, to Antwerp and Rotterdam, were terminated in June 1957. Grand Union then became increasingly dependant on its parent company, who began to almost monopolise its ships, even blocking other and probably more remunerative charters, claiming that it needed them itself. The writing appeared to be on the wall for Grand Union's independent existence, although its death was protracted. In 1960 and 1964 the immediate post-war new buildings, *Knebworth* and *Bosworth*, were sold, like all the company's sales going on to trade further for new owners. In February 1965 the remaining two vessels, *Marsworth* (3) and *Blisworth* (2), were transferred to General Steam Navigation Co. Ltd. and the fleet of the Grand Union (Shipping) Co. Ltd. became extinct.

Posthumous career

The fleet might have gone, but the Grand Union company was to be born again.[15] When General Steam decided to dip its toe into the exciting waters of container shipping, Grand Union (Shipping) Ltd. was taken out of cold storage and on 1st September 1967 its name was changed to European Unit Routes Ltd. Thrice-weekly services between Number 43 berth in Tilbury and the Waalhaven in Rotterdam began on 15th January 1968, using a ship that seems laughably small by today's standards, with a capacity of just 33 TEU. Services were later extended to Antwerp (Churchill Dock), Dunkirk, Zeebrugge and Hamburg. European Unit Routes owned no ships, but made use of chartered tonnage, some of it from other parts of the P&O Group. All were given names of species of deer to give the impression of speed, including *Caribou, Eland, Fallow Deer, Impala, Roe Deer,* and *Sassaby.*[16]

Parent company P&O was particularly prone to the disease whose symptoms included reorganisation of its operations according to the current theories fashionable amongst management consultants, and in April 1976 European Unit Routes Ltd. was dissolved. It had operated in much the same area as its small but unique canal-owned predecessor, but its chartered motor container ships provided a stark contrast to the original steamers of the Grand Union (Shipping) Ltd.

Incidents and accidents

The Grand Union's ships escaped major damage during the war, although there were casualties amongst its seagoing personnel. The company's minute books record that Captain Evans and a fireman named Keith of the *Marsworth* were missing since 10th May 1941 and were believed to have been drowned, but frustratingly there are no details of how this happened, and there is no record of the ship being attacked at this date.

On 9th March 1945 *Eskwood* was captured by a German raiding party at Granville in France where she had been discharging coal from Swansea. Her Master, Captain Wright, was shot dead whilst resisting capture during the raid. *Eskwood* was forced to sail to St. Helier, Jersey where she was loaded with huge concrete blocks, it is believed in readiness for an attempt to block Granville harbour.[17] The war ended before the attempt could be made.

Wartime wrecks were a continuing hazard, and on 25th June 1946 the *Knebworth*, on only her second voyage, struck submerged wreckage off the Nore and had to put back into the Thames, berthing near Gravesend.[18] In the busy waters where the Grand Union ships usually traded, collisions with other ships were not uncommon. On 31st December 1946 the *Marsworth* was inward bound from Antwerp with general cargo when she collided with the *Empire Treasure* (7,022/1943) near the Ovens Buoy in Gravesend Reach, although the incident did not result in serious damage.[19]

The only total loss sustained by Grand Union was the second *Marsworth*. On 26th November 1953 she collided with the French steamer *Larrivet* in dense fog and sank off Winterton in Norfolk. Fortunately, there were no casualties.

An incident concerning the *Bosworth* had more serious consequences in terms of loss of life. On 22nd December 1957 during a voyage from Granton to Porsgrunn in Norway with 700 tons of coke she hove to in a gale in position 56.54 north, 02.40 east and developed a serious list.[20] At 3.15pm GMT *Bosworth* sent out a Mayday

Narva at Preston. She diverted to go to the aid of *Bosworth* in a gale during 22nd December 1957, but later that day foundered herself. *[World Ship Society Ltd.]*

signal, to which a host of vessels responded, including at least five trawlers, a Blue Funnel cargo liner, a British Petroleum tanker, plus British, Finnish, German and Swedish North Sea traders, although most of these resumed their former course once it was clear that help was at hand for *Bosworth*. Soon after 8.00pm the steam trawler *Wolverhampton Wanderers* (536/1946) and the motor ship *Finnmerchant* (5,392/1953) were in sight, at which point the *Bosworth's* crew decided to abandon her, lowering a boat from which they were picked up safely by the trawler just before midnight. *Wolverhampton Wanderers* reported that the *Bosworth* was listing up to 25 degrees and was holed on her starboard quarter. Nevertheless, the crew of another trawler, *Faraday* (538/1947), saw a chance of salvage, and four men went on board the next day and, after several attempts, got a line on board and took her in tow. A convoy consisting of *Faraday*, *Bosworth* and *Wolverhampton Wanderers* berthed at Aberdeen about midnight on 23rd December. There must have been mixed emotions amongst the crews: those from *Bosworth* pleased to be safe yet wondering if they had abandoned their vessel prematurely, whilst the *Faraday's* crew would be looking forward to celebrating

what would undoubtedly be a well-deserved claim for salvage. However, there was a tragic sequel to the rescue.

One of the ships which had responded to *Bosworth's* distress signals was the steamer *Narva* (1,991/1944) of Glen and Company, Glasgow, on a voyage from Hudiksvall and other Swedish ports to Methil and Grangemouth with a cargo of wood pulp. From position 57.28 north, 03.00 east, *Narva* herself sent out a signal that she was sinking. Some of the vessels that responded to *Bosworth's* Mayday now headed for *Narva's* position, the first to arrive being the Bergen Line's turbine steamer *Leda* (6,670/1952). *Leda* launched a boat which approached *Narva*, the boat's crew suggesting to those huddled on *Narva's* deck that they jump clear. The suggestion was declined and the boat returned to *Leda*, whose officers then watched the *Narva* disappear from their radar screen. The Glasgow steamer appears to have launched a life raft or a boat, but her crew of 22 were never found despite searches of the area by ships and by aircraft from both the UK and Norway. It will never be known whether the *Narva* got into trouble because she was going to *Bosworth's* aid, but her loss is testimony to the ferocity of the gale that December day.

The steam trawlers *Wolverhampton Wanderers* (left) and *Faraday* (right) both went to the assistance of the *Bosworth*. *[World Ship Society Ltd.]*

Nomenclature

The first ship bought by the company was renamed after a significant location on the Grand Union Canal. To maintain the style, names chosen for the ships bought or ordered by Grand Union (Shipping) Co. Ltd. were taken from towns and villages in the English Midlands ending in 'worth', although not all had connections with the canal. When the company was choosing names for a new building in 1945, also considered were Kenilworth and Rickmansworth, the latter town certainly having a strong link to the canal. As apparent from the names used by the Newcastle tramp ship owner R.S. Dalgleish, there were plenty of names to chose from on this theme.

Blisworth A village in Northamptonshire where the Grand Union Canal Company's predecessors built a five-storey warehouse. Nearby Blisworth Tunnel is, at 3,056 yards, one of the longest canal tunnels currently in use.

Bosworth There are several villages of this name in Leicestershire. Husbands Bosworth is on the Grand Union Canal near Market Haborough. Better known is Market Bosworth on the Ashby Canal, close to Bosworth Field, the site of a battle in 1485 at which Henry Tudor defeated Richard III who famously lost both his crown and his life. He was the last English monarch to lead an army in battle.

Kilworth North and South Kilworth are Leicestershire villages, not far from the Grand Union Canal.

Knebworth Knebworth is in Hertfordshire, just south of Stevenage. There are no canals nearby.

Marsworth A village on the Grand Union Canal in Buckinghamshire where there is a flight of seven locks, a series of reservoirs and the Aylesbury Arm joins the main canal. As the name chosen for the Grand Union's first ship, it had special resonance and was used three times, even after the second ship named *Marsworth* sank.

Notes

1. A number of canal companies had tugs, including substantial ones in the case of the Manchester Ship Canal Company but, as far as the authors are aware, none had any vessels which routinely went to sea. Even the canal companies that built their own sea ports, as at Goole, Ellesmere Port and Runcorn, left it to others to run ships from their docks.

2. Minute books of the Grand Union Canal Carrying Co. Ltd. are held at the Waterways Archives, Gloucester. The authors are grateful for further information from Robin Craig (a former employee) and Clive Guthrie, both sadly no longer with us. See also Faulkner, A. 'The Regent's Canal: London's Hidden Waterway' (Waterways World, Burton-on-Trent, 2005).

3. The canal companies which merged were the Regent's Canal (whose Chairman W.H. Curtis appears to have suggested the amalgamation), the Grand Junction Canal, the Birmingham and Warwick Junction, the Warwick and Napton, and the Warwick and Birmingham Canals. As part of the amalgamation scheme, the Regent's Canal had purchased the three Warwick canals in 1927. This and other details are from the late Edward Paget-Tomlinson's prodigious work 'The Illustrated History of Canal and River Navigations' (Sheffield Academic Press, 1993).

4. The Leicester Navigation, the Loughborough Navigation and the Erewash Canal.

5. 'Grand Union Canal (including Regent's Canal Dock) and Associated Companies.' Publicity booklet, 1939.

6. Regent's Canal Dock was originally a four-acre basin at Limehouse completed in 1820, and entered from the Thames by a lock 125 by 31 feet. The Dock and its entrances were progressively enlarged, the 350 foot entrance being opened in 1869. Regent's Canal Dock was closed to commercial traffic in 1969.

7. *Merwede* was one of a number of steam coasters built by Dutch yards as a speculation during the First World War, her builder on the Koningsdiep canal near Groningen hoping to sell her to British owners who were desperate to replace war losses. However, she was not finished when, after the war, freight rates fell disastrously and with them the value of coasters, and after her launch she was laid up, incomplete. A Captain

Krans bought her in 1924 and had her completed, according to some sources at the yard of Scheepsbouwwerf De Merwede at Hardinxveld.

8. Parliamentary evidence of John Miller for the 1943 Grand Union Bill.

9. 'Lloyd's Register' for 1937 lists several possible candidates: a Swedish steamer (1,261/1922), a Danish steamer (844/1921), and an ex-British steam coaster then owned in Estonia (454/1904).

10. The Board minute book of Grand Union (Shipping) Ltd. for 1937 to 1956 is held by the National Maritime Museum as GSN/24/2.

11. A minute book covering the period 1937 to 1956 is in the National Maritime Museum, Greenwich, reference GSN/24/2.

12. Details from John de S. Winser 'The D-Day Ships'. (World Ship Society, Kendal, 1994) and 'Coasters go to War' (Ships in Focus, Preston, 2009). *Marsworth* was not involved in Operation Neptune, and her Government charter ending in October 1944, when the war was far from over, may suggest the Ministry of War Transport was not entirely happy with her performance.

13. Initially a price of £53,700 is quoted in minute books, but this was later amended to £57,090.

14. This company was discussed briefly in Ships in Focus 'Record' 36, pages 202-3. In addition to some ageing steam coasters, it had two motor coasters, including the *Peterjon*, a converted trawler owned by the Regent Shipping Co. Ltd. It had close connections with Grand Union (Shipping) Ltd.; George Tom being at one time a director and shareholder, serving briefly as chairman, making an unsuccessful offer to buy the Grand Union company, and later acquiring its *Kilworth*.

15. This section based on 'A Short History of European Routes Limited', duplicated sheets produced by P&O's Information Service.

16. Nick Robins 'Birds of the Sea: 150 years of the General Steam Navigation Company', (McCall, Portishead, 2007).

17. Channel Islands Occupation Society 'Channel Islands Merchant Shipping 1940-1945' (Channel Islands Occupation Society, Jersey Branch, n.d.)

18. 'Lloyd's Weekly Casualty Reports', April-July 1946.

19. 'Lloyd's Weekly Casualty Reports', January-March 1946

20. 'Lloyd's Weekly Casualty Reports', October-December 1957

Merwede aground

This photograph was bought by one of the editors from the USA a couple of years back and came complete with details supplied by photographer or agency. Dated 18th December 1929, the caption informs us that the photo is of the 'Norwegian' steamer *Merwede* which, bound from Rotterdam to Newhaven with bricks, was tossed up on a beach near Seaford in the '82-mile-an-hour gales which had recently swept the coast of Europe, paralysing traffic and taking many lives'. It was only whilst hunting for photographs for this feature that its significance was realised. The ship is, in fact, Dutch, and was acquired by the Grand Union the Grand Union (Stevedoring and Warehousing) Co. Ltd. in 1937 and renamed *Marsworth*, being transferred to Grand Union (Shipping) Ltd. a year later. Perhaps a reader can tell us more about the storm, the grounding and refloating of *Merwede*. [J. and M. Clarkson collection]

Fleet list

1. MARSWORTH 1937-1949
O.N. 165566 366g 188n
131.6 x 23.2 x 11.5 feet
T. 3-cyl. by Botje, Ensing & Co., Groningen,
Netherlands.
1920: Launched by Jac. Smit, Vierverlaten,
Netherlands for his own account as
KONINGSDIEP and laid up.
1924: Sold to Hendrik J. Krans, Rotterdam.
1925: Completed as MERWEDE.
1937: Acquired by the Grand Union (Stevedoring
and Warehousing) Co. Ltd., London and renamed
MARSWORTH.
1938: Transferred to Grand Union (Shipping) Ltd.,
London.
1949: Sold to Hindusthan Shipping Co. Ltd. (Juan
R. Mukherjee, manager), Calcutta, India and
renamed BAITARANI.
1957: Renamed SAVITRI
25.6.1960: Foundered in heavy weather near Shortt
Island, Dhamra Estuary, Chandbali, Orissa whilst
on a voyage from Calcutta to Chandbali with
general cargo.

2. BLISWORTH (1) 1939-1950
O.N. 113519 776g 348n
207.5 x 30.4 x 12.0 feet
T. 3-cyl. by Ross and Duncan, Govan.
12.3.1902: Launched by the Ailsa Shipbuilding Co.
Ltd., Ayr (Yard No.65).
4.1902: Completed for J. Milligen and Co. Ltd.,
Belfast as KATHLEEN.
12.1939: Acquired by Grand Union (Shipping)
Ltd., London and renamed BLISWORTH.
1.1950: Sold to the Holderness Steamship Co. Ltd.,
Hull for £8,000 and renamed HOLDERNIDD.
13.1.1956: Delivered to C.W. Dorkin and Co. for
breaking up at Redhaugh.

3. KILWORTH 1944-1950
O.N. 128813 803g 378n
201.8 x 30.0 x 11.6 feet
T. 3-cyl. by Blair and Co. Ltd., Stockton-on-Tees;
132 NHP, 600 IHP, 10 knots.
25.7.1911: Launched by W. Harkess and Son Ltd.,
Middlesbrough (Yard No. 189).
30.8.1911: Registered in the ownership of the
Meteor Steamship Co. Ltd. (R.A. Constantine
and T.H. Donking, managers), Middlesbrough as
ESKWOOD
1918: Sold to E. Johnson and Co. Ltd., Goole.
1926: Sold to S. and R. Steamships Ltd. (Stone and
Rolfe Ltd., managers), Llanelli.
1937: Sold to the Mersey Ports Stevedoring Co.
Ltd., Liverpool.
1944: Acquired by Grand Union (Shipping) Ltd.,
London.
15.2.1946: Renamed KILWORTH.
20.3.1950: Sold to George A. Tom and Co. Ltd.,
managers), London for £9,000.
6.4.1950: Transferred to the Fenchurch Shipping
Co. Ltd. (George A. Tom and Co. Ltd., managers),
London.
1951: Renamed FENCHURCH.
1951: Sold to the Holderness Steamship Co. Ltd.,
Hull and renamed HOLDERNOLL.
20.1.1956: Arrived at Gateshead to be broken up by
J.J. King and Co. Ltd.

Grand Union's first steamer, the Dutch-built *Marsworth, bought in 1937. [Newall Dunn collection]*

Blisworth (1) arriving at Preston from Garston on 12th October 1949. After loading a cargo of pitch she sailed for St Malo early on 14th October. *[J. and M. Clarkson collection]*

The veteran steamer *Kilworth* was acquired in 1944 as *Eskwood* and not renamed until 1946. *[Fotoflite incorporating Skyfotos]*

The company's first new building, the motor coaster *Knebworth* was ordered from Burntisland late in 1944, but delivered only in June 1946. *[Fotoflite incorporating Skyfotos]*

4. KNEBWORTH 1946-1960

O.N. 180871 857g 457n
183.0 x 31.7 x 12.9 feet
Oil engines 2SCSA 4-cyl. by British Polar Engines Ltd., Glasgow; 65 NHP, 690 BHP, 10 knots.
16.2.1946: Launched by the Burntisland Shipbuilding Co. Ltd., Burntisland (Yard No. 302)
22.5.1946: Registered in the ownership of Grand Union (Shipping) Ltd., London as KNEBWORTH.
6.1946: Completed.
30.11.1959: Sold to the Limerick Steamship Co. Ltd., Limerick for £33,000 and later renamed DROMINEER.

1964: Sold to Harold B. Dawe Ltd., St Johns, Newfoundland, Canada and renamed DOMINO RUN.
1974: Sold to Domino Run Steamship Co. Ltd., Piraeus, Greece and registered in Georgetown, Cayman Islands.
1979: Renamed MINO although no owner recorded.
4.1998: Deleted from 'Lloyd's Register' as continued existence in doubt.
Reported as being seized at Tripoli 1.1979, and was probably broken up locally in the 1980s.

5. BOSWORTH 1946-1964

O.N. 180944 865g 455n
192.4 (183.0) x 31.7 x 13.7 feet

Oil engines 2SCSA 4-cyl. by British Polar Engines Ltd., Glasgow; 65 NHP, 690 BHP, 850 IHP, 10 knots.
18.2.1946: Launched by the Burntisland Shipbuilding Co. Ltd., Burntisland (Yard No. 304).
28.8.1946: Registered in the ownership of Grand Union (Shipping) Ltd., London as BOSWORTH.
9.1946: Completed.
15.9.1964: Sold to Valier Bouchard, Rivière du Loup, Quebec, Canada for £40,000.
19.1.1965: Abandoned after grounding on St. Pierre Island, Miquelon whilst on a voyage from Sydney, Nova Scotia to Bonavista with coal.
27.1.1966: Register closed.

Bosworth on the Thames in 1954. *[Ships in Focus]*

6. MARSWORTH (2) 1949-1953

O.N. 181793 519g 238n 623d
156.7 x 27.6 x 9.2 feet
Oil engine 2SCSA 7-cyl. by
Crossley Brothers Ltd., Manchester;
465 BHP, 560 IHP, 10 knots.
3.2.1947: Launched by Charles
Hill and Sons Ltd., Bristol (Yard
No. 347).
22.11.1947: Registered
in the ownership of the
Williamstown Shipping Co.
Ltd. (Comben Longstaff and
Co. Ltd., managers), London as
SOMERSETBROOK.
25.7.1949: Acquired by Grand
Union (Shipping) Ltd., London
for £51,250.
5.8.1949: Renamed MARSWORTH.
26.11.1953: Sank in position
52.47 north, 01.44 east following
a collision in dense fog with
the French steamer LARRIVET
(3,754/1921) off Winterton
whilst on a voyage from London
to Stornoway with a cargo of
cement.
20.2.1954: Register closed.

Comben Longstaff's *Somersetbrook* (top) became the second *Marsworth* (middle) in 1949, but was lost in 1953. *[National Museum of Wales; World Ship Society Ltd.]*
Photographed leaving Swansea (bottom), Hughes Holden's *Brier Rose* became the third and last *Blisworth* in 1954. *[National Maritime Museum, P51881]*

7. MARSWORTH (3) 1954-1965

O.N. 168593 626g 318n
176.6 x 30.2 x 10.9 feet
Oil engine 4SCSA 6-cyl. by Mirrlees,
Bickerton and Day Ltd., Stockport; 10 knots.
4.11.1952: Launched by John Lewis and
Sons Ltd., Aberdeen (Yard No. 226).
12.1952: Completed for Hughes Holden
Shipping Ltd., Swansea as BRIER ROSE.
1954: Acquired by Grand Union
(Shipping) Ltd., London for £92,500 and
renamed MARSWORTH.
17.2.1965: Owners became the General
Steam Navigation Co. Ltd., London.
1969: Sold to Losinjska Plovidba, Rijeka,
Yugoslavia and renamed KIMEN.
1969: Owners became Brodogradiliste
'Cres', Cres, Yugoslavia.
1977: Owners became Brodogradiliste

The third *Marsworth* passes Tilbury inward bound. *[Ships in Focus]*

'Cres' Zanatsko Proizvadno i Usluzino Poduzece, Cres, Yugoslavia.
1991: Owners became the Flanonia Shipping Co. Ltd. (Brodogradiliste 'Cres' Zanatsko Proizvadno i Usluzino Poduzece, Cres, Croatia, managers) and placed under the flag of St. Vincent and the Grenadines.
22.10.1999: Arrived at Aliaga, Turkey.
3.11.1999: Breaking up began by Dortel Gemi Sokum Demir ve Celik San, Aliaga.

8. BLISWORTH (2) 1957-1965

O.N. 187686 1,031g 572n
213.0 x 33.1 x 14.1 feet
Oil engines 2SCSA 5-cyl. by British Polar Engines Ltd., Glasgow.
26.9.1957: Launched by Alexander Hall and Co. Ltd. Aberdeen (Yard No. 753) for Grand Union (Shipping) Ltd., London as BLISWORTH.
27.11.1957: Completed at a cost of £197,983.

17.2.1965: Owners became the General Steam Navigation Co. Ltd., London.
1971: Sold to Chesham Shipping Ltd. (Briggs Shipbrokers and Agents Ltd., managers), London and renamed FRANCES B.
1974: Sold to Lama Maritime Shipping Co. S.A.R.L., Beirut, Lebanon and renamed LEILA 1.
2.1.1987: Arrived at Tripoli, Lebanon to be broken up.
9.1987: Work began.

Blisworth in October 1962. *[J. and M. Clarkson]*

BOSUN'S LOCKER

Identification of photographs in 'Record' 48

48/01

The Bosun is guilty of not looking hard enough for this twin-funneled steamer in Laxon and Perry's book on British India. As several readers have pointed out, she is tucked away on page 214 as a unit of British India Associated Steamers, the *Eldorado* of 1873.

The 3,332 gross, iron hulled passenger steamer was built by Earle's Shipbuilding and Engineering Co. Ltd., Hull for the Indian services of Thomas Wilson, Sons and Co. Ltd. British India Associated Steamers acquired her and sister *Navarino* in 1877 and retained their names. *Eldorado* was transferred from Calcutta sailings to the Queensland mail service in 1883, but had returned to the London and Calcutta route when she was wrecked near Peniche in Portugal on 11th February 1885. Thanks also to Ian Farquhar, Tony Smythe, Bob Todd and John H. Wilterding.

48/02

A number of readers have told us that the two funnelled ship in the foreground of this Weymouth photograph is one of the Great Western Railway's trio built for the Channel Islands mail service by Laird Brothers at Birkenhead, *Antelope*, *Gazelle* or *Lynx* (all 672/1889), and that another of the trio is berthed astern of her. However, there is disagreement about which of the three appear in the photograph.

Geoff Holmes reckons that the photograph must have been taken during or before 1912 as by that date *Gazelle* (1908) and *Lynx* (1912) had been converted to cargo vessels and *Antelope* was sold in that year. Before the delivery in 1908 of passenger tenders all three had spent periods working as tenders at Plymouth and for this service their forward lifeboats were removed. According to J.H. Lucking's 'The Great Western at Weymouth', the *Antelope* was rarely seen at Weymouth after 1904. Geoff's guess is that the ship in the foreground is the *Lynx* and the vessel astern is *Gazelle* after her conversion to a cargo ship.

Jerzy Swieszkowski disagrees. Along with Robert Langlois, he notes that Hain's 1891-built, 2,437grt *Trevanion* (the ship alongside the quay) was sold to Greece in September 1911. He points out that *Antelope* was the only one of the GWR trio never to lose her passenger accommodation, although she tended to work mainly as a tender or as a relief ship, for instance taking over from August to October 1911 to cover for *Roebuck*, after which she operated between Plymouth and Nantes until the Great Western closed this service in 1912.

Lynx retained her passenger accommodation until 1912, but Jerzy believes that from 1903 she was mainly working as a tender out of Plymouth, and would not be seen back at Weymouth until she was converted to cargo only. The only member of the trio to have been converted to a cargo ship by September 1911 when *Trevanion* was sold was the *Gazelle*, and Jerzy identifies her as the vessel berthed astern, which has lost her forward lifeboats.

The complete set of boats on the vessel in the foreground (and *Lynx's* absence) tempts Jerzy to identify her as *Antelope*, and he postulates that the photograph was taken in August or early September 1911. Certainly the observation that the vessel is berthed outboard of the *Trevanion*, which has steam up, and that she is receiving attention from a man in a punt (and possibly having just received coal from a lighter), suggests that she was in service, and probably standing in for *Roebuck*.

Jerzy also provides the histories of the three ships. In August 1913 *Antelope* was sold to Greece as *Atromitos*, and broken up in 1933. After her 1908 conversion to cargo only, *Gazelle* worked mainly between Weymouth and the Channel Isles, work which was interrupted by serving as a minesweeper in the Mediterranean during the First World War. She was broken up in September 1925. *Lynx* also served in the Mediterranean, as HMS *Lynn*, and then returned to Weymouth until broken up, also in 1925.

Our correspondents have obviously done a great deal of detective work on this photograph, and we thank Geoff Holmes, Peter H. King, Robert Langlois, George Robinson, Tony Smythe and Jerzy Swieszkowsky.

48/03

Derek Atherton points out that the ship named 'SS *Excellent*' in this photograph has an unconvincing wood and canvas construction on her forecastle deck. The lifeboat falls are down to the water and there is a large warship with many spectators on deck in the background. The photo is also very tightly cropped.

He thinks it could be a staged event at Portsmouth in the years following the First World War showing a 'Q ship' in action. The lifeboat has departed with the panic party going over the side abandoning ship as the 'U boat' approaches her victim to sink her with gunfire. Is there a RN submarine out of view to the right ? The 'Q ship' is photographed the moment after the ensign has been hoisted, the guns have been exposed and the opening salvo has been fired with gun smoke projected to the side of the ship.

HMS *Excellent* was the chief school of naval gunnery at the shore establishment at Whale Island, Portsmouth which would have trained the gun crews for the Q ships. HMS *Excellent* had two Mersey class trawlers as tenders in the period following 1919, both named *Excellent*. They were the *William Leach* between 1919 and 1920 and *Andrew Jewer* which carried the name between 1922 and 1946. The photograph depicts one of these, both of which were built by Cochrane and Sons, Selby in 1918 and both of 324 grt. *William Leech* was sold in1922 retaining her name and became the French *Excellent* in the Second World War. *Andrew Jewer* was sold in 1946 and renamed *Malvern*.

Bob Todd dates the photograph to the early 1930s at one of Navy Days that were held at Portsmouth, usually over the August Bank Holiday. This would make the vessel the former *Andrew Jewer*.

Thanks also to Peter H. King and George Robinson.

48/04

Only Tony Smythe offers an opinion on this yacht, and he agrees with the Bosun that it is *Varuna*, built by A. and J. Inglis in 1897 for a Eugene Higgins, a substantial vessel of 1,573grt 300 feet overall.

More photographs for identification

49/01 and 49/02

A correspondent supplies two scans, at least one of which (49/01 bottom of previous page) is taken on the Mersey, and may show a White Star liner being coaled with a tender alongside. The combination of two funnels and three masts leads to a very tentative identification as either the *Teutonic* or *Majestic* of 1889.

49/02 (below) is a very similar looking ship, but has a whale-backed type poop, and probably a different funnel scheme. The paddle tug certainly has a distinctive funnel markings. Can anyone offer identifications?

49/03 (middle) is of a burnt out steamer but there is no indication as to her name and when or where the picture was taken. Although the card is marked 'British made' that doesn't mean to say she is in UK waters. There is a white line on her bow just above the anchors - maybe this could be a clue.

49/04 (bottom). This is a nice postcard of some sailing vessels and a steamer, the credit on the back reading: Love's, The Postcard House, Middlegate, Hartlepool. The steamer is the *Grovelea* (1,267 tons gross) completed as the the *Lady Furness* by the Blyth Shipbuilding and Dry Docks Co. Ltd. in 1906 for Alfred Christensen of Copenhagen. After passing through the hands of a further Danish owner and the British Maritime Trust Ltd. (Furness Withy and Co. Ltd.) she was sold to Rederi A/B Groveland (J.P. Jonson), Landskrona, Sweden in 1912 and renamed *Grovelea*. She only retained the name for three years as in 1915 she was purchased by the Gas, Light and Coke Co.Ltd., of London (Stephenson Clarke and Co., managers) and renamed *Phare*. Her time with them was brief, as she was torpedoed and sunk off Scarborough on 31st October 1917 whilst on passage from the Tyne to London with coal. There are at least six sailing vessels in the photo but, although the photo is extremely sharp, their names cannot be read. One of the nearest ships to her is registered Helsingborg. The name could be *Anders* but the bosun has not managed to find any details of her. Perhaps someone can identify the location and tell us more about the picture and the photographer. It was clearly taken between 1912 and 1915, and if it is at West Hartlepool, there is a surprising number of sailing vessels in port at this date.

ROBERTSON FOLLOW UP

'William Robertson and the Gem Line', published by Ships in Focus in late 2009, has been generally well received and the reviews have been positive. We were particularly gratified to hear from J.W. Simpson, son of the late Captain J.A. Simpson, whose reminiscences of working for Robertsons in the late 1940s were included in the book. Mr Simpson's voyages with his father are mentioned in this account, and he recalls being terribly seasick during his trip on the steamer *Fluor*.

As usual, a number of additions, comments and corrections have been received which we include here.

Additions

Dave Hocquard offers more details on the German career of the motor vessel *Spinel* (2), left behind in the Inner Basin at Dunkirk on 25th May 1940 when the lock gates had been destroyed by bombing. She appears to have suffered only minor damage from shrapnel and from some sabotage by her crew. Once the lock gates had been repaired, she was able to sail, and proceeded direct to Jersey with a full cargo of military vehicles which had been left behind by the British Expeditionary Force. She remained in Robertson colours for some time, with 'Glasgow' still painted on her stern. For the first few years of the war she was running supplies for both the civilian population and the Germans from Granville to Jersey and Guernsey with the odd trip to Alderney. It was only after D-Day in June 1944 when the Allies had total command of the seas around the Channel Islands that any German ship that moved was attacked. During this time she firstly helped to evacuate most of the forced labour on all the islands to France. She then moved heavy guns and equipment from Guernsey to Jersey to strengthen the so-far-undefended east coast of Jersey now that the French coast only 16 miles away was in US hands. But her luck held and she came through almost undamaged until finally laid up in St. Helier Harbour in late August 1944.

Ian Wilson identifies the location of the photograph of *Pearl* on the title page as Waterford, and suggests it might have been taken by John Anderson who traded as 'Spindrift Photos'. Ian also speculates that Hugh H. Smiley of Paisley, for whom William Robertson managed three iron steamers between 1885 and 1891, had connections with Larne. *Olderfleet* and *Latharna* were both named after places near Larne, whilst *Dalriada* is the old name for north Antrim. Ian also points out that the *Larry Bane*, which Roberstson bought from Belfast owners in 1888 and never renamed, was not, as might be expected, named after a person but after the quarry jetty near Larry Bane Head, North Antrim.

Corrections

Charles Waine rightly takes the authors to task for suggesting that the masts of the early Robertson steamers, and particularly *Diamond* (2) on page 40, were black. They were in fact brown varnished wood, as the highlights visible on the mast suggest. Only the top part of the mizzen was black, the varnished lower eight feet or so being separated by a narrow white band. Charles points out that the deckhouses on *Cairngorm* (2) on page 65, and indeed in other photographs, are not painted stone-colour but are wood panelled and carefully grained, and portholes are polished brass.

Charles also points out that the 1883-built *Cameo* (2) has a full-height forecastle, not a half-height one as the caption on page 9 claims.

Referring to 'walkways' in captions to photographs of *Fluor* (1) on page 2 and *Tourmaline* (2) on page 91 proved hazardous. *Tourmaline* happened to have a jetty behind her, which was mistakenly thought to be part of the ship. We are told the name 'gangway' is more appropriate; the term 'walkway' being reserved for the temporary way made by securing stanchions to the top of a timber cargo. Charles points out that gangways across the well deck were fairly standard on long raised-quarter deck coasters of the period, and in port were hauled up against the ratlines. The term ratlines is used on page 85 in the caption to *Pebble* (2), but in this instance these are, in fact, hardwood battens.

Nomenclature proved divisive in several other places. The oxymoronic term 'open wheelhouse' might be justified as post-modern irony, but Charles will not abide it. The description of the smoke outlet from the galley as a 'chimney' on page 98 is also controversial. Charles points out that all general arrangement drawings, including that of *Sphene* on the front end papers, have it labelled 'stove funnel', but research carried out in the field on an actual steamer found that a retired sea-going engineer unhesitating named such an outlet as a 'chimney'!

On page 98 *Jade* is described as having an exposed steering position, but this is, in fact, a compass platform.

Marchioness of Lorne

Page 6 noted that no steamer named *Marchioness of Lorne* could be identified around 1871, when Duckworth and Langmuir's 'Clyde and other Coastal Steamers' claimed she was operating a service to the Western Isles for Robertson. However, Fred Hawks has identified the likely vessel, built by J. and R. Swan at Maryhill in 1866 as *Swan* and of 56 grt. She was renamed *Marchioness of Lorne* in December 1871 when her main owner was D.D. Balfour. She was still in his ownership on 17th March 1875 when she was wrecked off Hainish Point, Tiree. Her final voyage, from Girvan to Tiree with coal and grain, supports Duckworth and Langmuir's claim about her service, but there is no evidence of Robertson's involvement in the vessel's ownership.

In Glasgow Upper Harbour

We are indebted to Ian Ramsay for sharing his recollections of two Robertson coasters which regularly visited the Upper Harbour at Glasgow

'This concerns the motor coasters *Prase* and *Cairngorm* and your mention on page 97 of the diminutive funnel and superstructure; and the obvious fact that the single mast is hinged in a tabernacle. In the immediate post-war years, both of these ships were occasional visitors to the Upper Harbour of Glasgow situated between King George V Bridge and Victoria Bridge – the upper limit of Clyde navigation. To reach the Upper Harbour berths vessels had to pass under King George V Bridge, the two railway bridges giving access to Glasgow Central Station and then the Glasgow, or Jamaica Bridge, all fixed and of fairly limited headroom. The Upper Harbour berths were only on the north bank of the river and extended from Jamaica Bridge to the Victoria or Stockwell Bridge and were divided about one third of the quay length by a fairly low-level, pedestrian suspension bridge.

The motor vessel *Cairngorm* of 1938 moves cautiously along the Clyde with her gear lowered ready to pass under the Glasgow bridges. *[Robertson archives]*

The easternmost berth, at Victoria Bridge, was occupied by the composite, sailing vessel *Carrick* (formerly *City of Adelaide*) - the RNVR (Scotland) Club Ship. Going westwards, the next berth was used by Warnock's and other puffers for discharging sand that had been dug from the sandbanks off Port Glasgow. From the sand berth to the suspension bridge, most of the quay was used by J. and A. Gardner's elderly steam coasters that had either brought granite products from their Bonawe quarries, or were laid up awaiting a cargo.

Between the suspension bridge and Jamaica Bridge there was only one berth in use and it was immediately downstream from the former and that was the one used by Robertson's *Prase* and *Cairngorm*. I do not know what the cargo was but it was a snow white, fine powder and was only discharged when there was no likelihood of rain. It certainly looked like a processed lime derivative but whether for building work, agriculture or what, I do not know. The cargo was grab-discharged by an electric, dockside crane which, unusually, dropped its load through a square hatch in the roof of the dock shed which was also quickly closed with the onset of any rain. So, indeed, the two ships had their low air draft used on occasions!

I believe the Gardner ships, when arriving loaded, found it quite a challenge in reaching their berths as there was not a lot of water under the bridges at low tide which necessitated getting under the lowest bridge at about half, but not too much, tide in case the ship's air draught was too great. Similarly, when leaving after discharge, they had to be able to ballast the ship into a near-level trim and again compute between height of tide, depth of water and bridge clearance. *Prase* and *Cairngorm* had the same difficulties but theirs was compounded by the fact that they had to turn in the river in the short length between the suspension bridge and Jamaica Bridge.

I remember seeing one of Gardner's motor coaster in the Upper Harbour with the upper half of the wheelhouse and the large hand steering wheel dismantled. In looking at it, I was not sure if the removal had been deliberate or as a result of striking a bridge arch. Needless to say, I did not think it politic to ask!

Another neat little motor coaster that regularly appeared from about 1950 and visited regularly for a number of years, was ICI's *Polythene*. As she was quite small, I assume that she probably came from the Manchester Ship Canal/River Weaver but I never heard what her cargo was or where she came from. [*Polythene* (330/1949) would most likely have come from ICI's alkali plant at Burn Naze, near Fleetwood with sodium hydroxide or sodium carbonate, both of which would have to be protected from rainwater. Quite possibly, *Prase* and *Cairngorm* were bringing similar cargoes. Ed.]

Apart from being a native of Renfrew, I wonder if William Robertson's coal and ship owning business owed its start to Renfrew's adjacency to the short spur from the Forth and Clyde Canal that came down to the Clyde opposite its confluence with the River Cart; all long before the move of the shipyard of J. and G. Thomson (later John Brown and Co.) to a green-field site that later became the town of Clydebank.'

Typographical errors

The ever-vigilant Bob Todd has spotted a few typographical errors.

Page 23: Table 4, the second requisition of *Felspar* ended on 26.5.1944 not 26.5.1940.

Page 24: Table 4 continued, the third requisition of *Dagmar* began on 20.6.1940.

A line was omitted from this table, which should read:

Empire Fanal	Store Ship (Military)	17.11.1944	17.12.1944
	Coasting and Short Sea Service	18.12.1944	1.8.1946

Page 36: *Cameo* was sold to William Fishwick and William Webber on 20.10.1897 not 20.7.1897.

Page 37: the cable ship in the *Jacinth* photograph is confirmed as the *Britannia* of 1885 in the period 1896-1907.

Page 38: the register closed date for *Amethyst* (2) should be 8.10.1908.

Page 45: the register closed date *Peridot* should be 1.12.1905.

Page 45, *Olivine* (1), then named *Yewdale*, was sold to William Postlethwaite on 22.4.1904.

Page 49: details of requisition of *Spinel* (1) should read:

26.8.1914: Requisitioned by the British Government until 5.10.1915.

6.10.1915: Commissioned as an Admiralty fleet messenger until 29.6.1920.

Page 57: the yard number of *Fluor* (1) should be 126.

Page 60: the register closed date for *Obsidian* (2) should be 17.3.1920.

Page 71: Breakers of *Amethyst* (3) in 5.1951 were W. Johnson and Co. at Stockton, California

Members of the Robertson family point out that John McKellar Robertson was promoted to captain in the RNVR in 1928, not 1918 (page 21). They add that he became Commanding Officer of the Clyde Division of the RNVR in 1930 and, as well as his OBE, he was awarded a CBE in 1937.

A 144-page, A4-size hardback, 'William Robertson and the Gem Line' remains available at £21.00 plus £3.50 post and packing from J. and M. Clarkson, 18 Franklands, Longton, Preston PR4 5PD, phone 01772 612855 or by e-mail: from *shipsinfocus@btinternet.com*

Pages 62 and 63 of 'William Robertson and the Gem Line' described the grounding of *Onyx* (3) of 1904 at Llanddulas on 12th February 1907 and her subsequent salvage. Alan Savory has very kindly lent us postcards from his collection showing the lightening operation which was necessary before *Onyx* could be refloated on 27th February. The photograph above was probably taken after the middle and upper photographs on page 63 as it shows sheer legs in position forward as well as chutes amidships. The large number of horses present suggests that her limestone cargo was being carted away as it was shovelled out of her holds. The mound built up amidships is, presumably, material from the beach. It is a fascinating reflection on Edwardian society that so many photographs were taken of a relatively minor incident, and that several were turned into commercial postcards. *[Alan Savory collection]*

Nektarios and Emmanouil Papadakis sent this photograph which almost certainly shows a Robertson coaster in a Greek or Turkish port. Five members of the fleet were requisitioned as Fleet Messengers during the First World War, and presumably sent out

to work in the Eastern Mediterranean. *Turquoise* (1) and *Nugget* (2) were lost soon after setting out. *Asteria* (1) can be ruled out as her foremast was stepped half way between her bridge and forecastle. *Pebble* (1) and *Spinel* (1) are both possible, but are virtually indistinguishable, both being built by Scotts of Bowling, although *Spinel* was ten feet longer. The No.9 is no help, as no Robertson ship carried this

number, and there is ample evidence that painting of such numbers did not correlate with the numbers officially allocated to requisitioned vessels. *Spinel* returned home, but *Pebble*, was still under Admiralty requisition whilst at Mudros in November 1919 when she was abandoned as a constructive total loss, but was patched up and worked for Greek owners until lost by fire and explosion in 1933.

SOURCES AND ACKNOWLEDGEMENTS

We thank all who gave permission for their photographs to be used, and for help in finding photographs we are particularly grateful to Tony Smith, Jim McFaul and David Whiteside of the World Ship Photo Library; to Ian Farquhar, F.W. Hawks, Peter Newall, William Schell; and to David Hodge and Bob Todd of the National Maritime Museum, and other museums and institutions listed.

Research sources have included the *Registers* of William Schell and Tony Starke, 'Lloyd's Register', 'Lloyd's Confidential Index', 'Lloyd's Shipping Index', 'Lloyd's War Losses', 'Mercantile Navy Lists', 'Marine News', 'Sea Breezes' and 'Shipbuilding and Shipping Record'. Use of the facilities of the World Ship Society, the Guildhall Library, the National Archives and Lloyd's Register of Shipping and the help of Dr Malcolm Cooper are gratefully acknowledged. Particular thanks also to Heather Fenton for editorial and indexing work, and to Marion Clarkson for accountancy services.

THE CLIPPER FAMILY OF REEFER VESSELS
Part 3
Tony Breach

Wild Flamingo in Federal colours with her original white, if somewhat rust-streaked, hull. *[FotoFlite incorporating Skyfotos]*

Fleet list entries are in the usual Ships in Focus style. Unless stated otherwise, the flag of the vessel is that of the owning company, the first name in the ownership entry. Names of beneficial owners, where known, are given in brackets before those of the managers.

SUPER CLIPPERS

Built by Drammen Slip and Verksted, Drammen, Norway

Yard No.76 **WILD FLAMINGO**
O.N. 360873 IMO 7325710 6,925/5,014g
3,834/2,700n 9,750d
144.76 x 134.75 x 18.00 x 11.61 metres
Refrigerated capacity: 381,475 cubic feet
Sulzer 8RND68 2SCSA oil engine by Sulzer Brothers Ltd., Winterthur, Switzerland; 13,200 BHP, 23 knots.
21.6.1973: Launched for Federal Steam Navigation Co. Ltd. (P&O General Cargo Division), London) as WILD FLAMINGO.
25.10.1973: Completed.
23.5.1983: Sold to Sembawang Reefer Lines (Ciku) Private Ltd. (Sembawang Johnson Shipmanagement (Private) Ltd., Singapore)

and renamed REEFER CIKU.
1987: Transferred to Sembawang Reefer Lines (Duku) Bahamas Ltd., Nassau (Sembawang Shipping Co. Private Ltd., Singapore).
11.1987: Sold to Countach Shipping Co. Ltd.,

Limassol, Cyprus (Bulkserve Shipping Co. Ltd.) (Enias Shipping Co. S.A., Piraeus) and renamed FRIO CHILE.
1990: Owners became Pineforest Shipping Co. Ltd., Limassol (Lomar Shipping Ltd., Piraeus).

Reefer Ciku was formerly the *Wild Flamingo* in Lauritzen colours. All four P & O 'Wilds' took 'Reefer' names after their sale. *[FotoFlite incorporating Skyfotos, 32557]*

1993: Transferred to Pacific-Sea Management Corporation, Panama and renamed LAS PALMAS.

1994: Reverted to Pineforest Shipping Co. Ltd., Limassol (Lomar Shipping Ltd., Piraeus) and renamed FRIO CHILE.

4.1.1995: Abandoned west of Honshu in position 38.22 north, 150.58 east after taking on water during a voyage from Callao to Hachinohe via Honolulu with a cargo of frozen squid. Two crew members were lost but 25 survivors were rescued by NEPTUNE CORUNDUM (IMO 8204468, 35,084/1984).

8.1.1995: Sank in position 38.56 north, 151.36 east.

Yard No.77 WILD FULMAR

O.N. 363183 IMO 7369015 6,925/5,014g
3,840/2,706n 9,750d
144.76 x 134.75 x 18.01 x 11.61 metres
Refrigerated capacity: 381,467 cubic feet
Sulzer 8RDN68 2SCSA oil engine by Sulzer Brothers Ltd., Winterthur, Switzerland; 13,200 BHP, 23 knots.

27.11.1973: Launched for Federal Steam Navigation Co. Ltd. (P&O General Cargo Division), London) as WILD FULMAR.

7.3.1974: Completed.

3.5.1983: Sold to Sembawang Reefer Lines (Duku) Private Ltd. (Sembawang Johnson Shipmanagement (Private) Ltd., Singapore) and renamed REEFER DUKU.

1987: Transferred to Sembawang Reefer Lines (Duku) Bahamas Ltd., Nassau, Bahamas (Sembawang Shipping Co. Private Ltd., Singapore).

1.1988: Sold to Manifest Shipping Co. Ltd., Limassol, Cyprus (Kappa Maritime Ltd., London) and renamed STARSEA.

23.5.1990: Following an explosion and fire

Wild Fulmar with P&O's corn-coloured hull and Federal's funnel colours. *[FotoFlite incorporating Skyfotos, 372216]*

in engine room abandoned 35 miles north west of Punta Mala on the Pacific coast of Panama during a voyage from Corinto to Zeebrugge.

1.6.1990: Arrived Balboa under tow and subsequently sold to Paul Cheng Ltd. (Trans Globe Marine Ltd.), Hong Kong.

28.7.1991: Left Balboa as MIDWAY under the St. Vincent flag in tow of tug ATLANTIC RESCUER (IMO 6926048, 662/1969).

22.2.1992: Arrived Alang, India for demolition.

13.3.1993: Work commenced by Esoofbhai at Khanbhai.

The legal fight over the vessel's insurance

continued for several years with underwriters declining to pay compensation and the dispute finally reached the House of Lords in London.

Yard No.78 FRIGOARTICO

IMO 7383061 7,148/5,426g 4,322/2,770n 9,736d
144.76 x 134.75 x 18.00 x 11.64 metres
Refrigerated capacity: 381,467 cubic feet
Sulzer 8RND68 2SCSA oil engine by Sulzer Brothers Ltd., Winterthur, Switzerland; 13,200 BHP, 23.25 knots.

5.4.1974: Launched for TRANSFRUTA-Companhia Nacional de Navios Frigorificos SarL (Companhia Nacional de Navegacao),

Frigoartico in her original owners' colours. *[FotoFlite incorporating Skyfotos, 282934]*

Lisbon, Portugal as FRIGOARTICO.
7.1974: Completed.
1982: Sold to Star Determination Shipping
Corporation, Panama (Portline – Transportes
Maritimos Internacionais SarL, Lisbon and
renamed CAP FRIO.
1985: Transferred to Portline – Transportes
Maritimos Internacionais SarL, Lisbon and
renamed TROPICAL SINTRA.
Subsequently sold to Intercontinental
Transportation Services and OCP (Atlantic)
Ltd., Monrovia, Liberia (Dole Fresh Fruit
International Ltd., San Jose).
1993: Owners restyled Talita Shipping Ltd.,
Monrovia (Dole Fresh Fruit International
Ltd., San Jose).
1998: Transferred to Tropical Navigation
(Malta) Ltd., Valeta, Malta (Dole Fresh Fruit
International Ltd., San Jose).
3.6.1999: Arrived Alang, India for demolition.

Yard No.79 **FRIGOANTARTICO**
IMO 7383073 7,148/5,426g 4,322/2,770n
9,735d
144.75 x 134.74 x 18.00 x 11.64 meters
Refrigerated capacity: 381,714 cubic feet
Sulzer 8RND68 2SCSA oil engine by Sulzer
Brothers Ltd., Winterthur, Switzerland;
13,200 BHP, 23.25 knots.
6.9.1974: Launched for TRANSFRUTA-
Companhia Nacional de Navios Frigorificos
SarL (Companhia Nacional de Navegacao),
Lisbon, Portugal as FRIGOANTARTICO.
12.1974: Completed.
1984: Sold to Star Contract Shipping
Corporation, Panama (Portline – Transportes
Maritimos Internacionais SarL, Lisbon) and
renamed CAP FERRATO.
1985: Transferred to Portline – Transportes
Maritimos Internacionais SarL, Lisbon and
renamed TROPICAL ESTORIL.
Subsequently sold to Intercontinental
Transportation Services and OCP (Atlantic)
Ltd., Monrovia, Liberia.
1993: Transferred to Dole Fresh Fruit
International Ltd., San Jose, Costa Rica
under the Liberian flag.
1998: Transferred to Tropical Navigation
(Malta) Ltd., Valletta, Malta (Dole Fresh
Fruit International Ltd., San Jose).
7.6.2001: Arrived Alang, India for
demolition.

Yard No.81 **IFNI**
IMO 7383097 7,563g 4,215n 9,735d
144.76 x 134.75 x 18.00 x 11.64 metres
Refrigerated capacity: 385,534 cubic feet
Sulzer 8RND68 2SCSA oil engine by Sulzer
Brothers Ltd., Winterthur, Switzerland;
13,200 BHP, 23 knots.
11.7.1975: Launched for Compagnie
Marocaine de Navigation COMANAV,
Casablanca, Morocco as IFNI.
11.1975: Completed.
1992: Sold to Channel Maritime Co.
Ltd., Valletta, Malta (International Reefer
Services S.A., [Costas Comninos], Piraeus,
Greece) and renamed BRASILIA REEFER.
10.6.2000: Arrived Mumbai, India for
demolition.

Frigoantartico. (FotoFlite incorporating Skyfotos)

The Moroccan *Ifni.* [FotoFlite incorporating Skyfotos, 17355]

Ifni as *Brasilia Reefer.* [FotoFlite incorporating Skyfotos, 134477]

Top: *Imilchil* in Compagnie Marocaine de Navigation colours. *[FotoFlite incorporating Skyfotos, 11764]*

Middle: *Emanuel*. Note the revised funnel design and modified cargo gear. *[FotoFlite incorporating Skyfotos, 333990]*

Bottom: *Emanuel* as *Emanuel B* in Lauritzen colours. *[FotoFlite incorporating Skyfotos, 78629]*

Opposite top: *Emanuel* again as the *UB Prince*. Note the Ugland Brothers' funnel colours. *[FotoFlite incorporating Skyfotos, 239482]*

Yard No.82 IMILCHIL

IMO 7383102 7,563g 4,215n 9,634d
144.76 x 134.75 x 18.00 x 11.64 metres
Refrigerated capacity: 386,841 cubic feet
Sulzer 8RND68 2SCSA oil engine by Sulzer
Brothers Ltd., Winterthur, Switzerland;
13,200 BHP, 23 knots.
4.12.1975: Launched for Compagnie
Marocaine de Navigation COMANAV,
Casablanca, Morocco as IMILCHIL.
12.3.1976: Completed.
19.8.1990: Taken in tow and crew evacuated
after engine room flooded during a voyage
from Cristobal to Northern Europe.
26.9.1990: Arrived in tow at Cristobal where
she was subsequently abandoned to salvors
and eventually sold to Hong Kong interests
for demolition.
1.8.1992: Left Cristobal in tow of Maltese
tug PACIFIC RESCUER (834/1962) for
Pakistani breakers.
1.11.1992: Arrived Tema and grounded in
the anchorage.
1998: Reported as still grounded at Tema
Quarantine Anchorage and offered for sale
to local breakers.

Yard No.83 EMANUEL

IMO 7411349 6,993/5,072g 3,795/2,616n
9,612d
144.2 x 133.76 x 17.99 x 11.61 metres
Refrigerated capacity: 395,413 cubic feet
Sulzer 8RND68 2SCSA oil engine by Sulzer
Brothers Ltd., Winterthur, Switzerland;
13,200 BHP, 22.75 knots.
11.5.1976: Launched for A/S Shipping
Enchant (Peter Y. Berg, trading as Berg
and Bugge Reefers), Drammen, Norway as
EMANUEL.
30.9.1976: Completed.
Prior to 1983: Transferred to Polar Shipping
(Private) Ltd. (Berg and Bugge Reefers
(Private) Ltd., Singapore.
1985: Sold to Costa de Marfil Compania
Naviera S.A., Panama (Leandros Shipping
Co. S.A. Panama [Diamantis Pateras Ltd.,
London]) and renamed EMANUEL B under
the Bahamas flag.
1990: Sold to Rex Compania Naviera
S.A., Nassau, Bahamas (Transcontinental
Maritime and Trading S.A., [Comninos
Brothers], Piraeus, Greece).
1994: Sold to United Discovery S.A.,
Panama (Castle Shipholding S.A.. Piraeus)
and renamed EMANUEL C under the

Bahamas flag.
1995: Sold to A/S Gerrards Rederi,
Kristiansand, Norway (Ugland Brothers Ltd.
Egham, Surrey) and renamed UB PRINCE.
1997: Transferred to UB Shipping Ltd.,
Georgetown, Cayman and flag changed to
Bahamas.
2002: Sold to Saudi Cold Store Co. Ltd.,
Jeddah, Saudi Arabia and renamed TBREED
VII.
2004: Reported broken up.

Yard No.84 WILD GANNET

O.N. 377183 IMO 7411351 6,933/5,017g
3,796/2,639n 9,592d
144.76 x 134.78 x 18.00 x 11.64 metres
Refrigerated capacity: 381,467 cubic feet
Sulzer 8RND68 2SCSA oil engine by Sulzer
Brothers Ltd., Winterthur, Switzerland;
13,200 BHP, 23 knots.
18.10.1976: Launched for Midland Gillett
Leasing (South) Ltd. (Federal Steam
Navigation Co. Ltd., lessees) (P&O
General Cargo Division), London as WILD
GANNET.
4.2.1977: Completed.
30.3.1983: Sold to Sembawang Reefer
Lines (Manggis) Private Ltd. (Sembawang
Johnson Shipmanagement Private
Ltd.), Singapore and renamed REEFER
MANGGIS.
1986: Transferred to Sembawang Reefer
Lines (Bahamas) Ltd., Nassau (Sembawang
Johnson Shipmanagement Private Ltd.,
Singapore).
1990: Sold to Marine Liberation S.A.,
Panama (International Reefer Services S.A.
[Costas Comninos]), Piraeus, Greece) and
renamed IONIC REEFER.
1997: Renamed VERGINA REEFER
23.3.1998: Laid-up at Eleusis.
1999: Transferred to Morcate Marine Inc.,
Monrovia, Liberia (International Reefer
Services S.A. [Costas Comninos], Piraeus)
13.7.2002: Arrived at Aliaga, Turkey
in tow from Eleusis for demolition by
Karahuseyinoglu Demir Celik Ltd.

Above: *Wild Gannet* in P&O livery. *[FotoFlite incorporating Skyfotos]*
Below: *Wild Gannet* as *Ionic Reefer* after sale to Comninos. *[David Whiteside collection]*

Yard No.85 **WILD GREBE**
O.N. 377491 IMO 7411363
6,933/5,017g 3,835/2,641n 9,592d
144.46 x 134.78 x 18.00 x 11.64
metres
Refrigerated capacity: 382,456 cubic
feet
Sulzer 8RND68 2SCSA oil engine
by Sulzer Brothers Ltd., Winterthur,
Switzerland; 13,200 BHP, 22.75
knots.
15.10.1977: Launched for Federal
Steam Navigation Co. Ltd., London
(P&O General Cargo Division,
London) as WILD GREBE.
31.1.1978: Completed.
29.4.1983: Sold to Sembawang
Reefer Lines (Nangka) Private
Ltd. (Sembawang Johnson
Shipmanagement (Private) Ltd.),
Singapore and renamed REEFER
NANGKA.
1986: Transferred to Sembawang
Reefer Lines (Bahamas) Ltd.,
Nassau (Sembawang Johnson
Shipmanagement (Private) Ltd.),
Singapore).
1990: Sold to Golden Liberation
S.A. (International Reefer Services
S.A. [Costas Comninos]), Piraeus,
Greece and renamed AEOLIC
REEFER.
1997: Transferred to Shore Lark
Marine Services S.A., Nassau,
Bahamas (International Reefer
Services S.A. [Costas Comninos],
Piraeus) and renamed MINOIC
REEFER
2003: Transferred to Linkfield S.A.,
Panama.
30.10.2003: Demolition commenced
by Indian breakers.

Yard No.86 **IMOUZZER**
IMO 7432239 7,178g 4,091n 9,138d
144.76 x 134.75 x 18.01 x 11.64
metres
Refrigerated capacity: 378,641 cubic
feet
Sulzer 8RND68 2SCSA oil engine
by Sulzer Bros Ltd., Winterthur;
13,200 BHP, 22.5 knots.
4.1977: Launched for Compagnie
Marocaine de Navigation,
COMANAV, Casablanca, Morocco
as IMOUZZER.
1991: Sold to Longnest Marine
Co. Ltd., Limassol, Cyprus
(International Reefer Services
S.A. [Costas Comninos], Piraeus,
Greece) and renamed TROPICANA
REEFER.
25.5.1998: Laid up at Eleusis.
2002: Transferred to Phoenix
Navigation S.A., Panama
(International Reefer Services S.A.
[Costas Comninos], Piraeus).
4.7.2002: Arrived at Aliaga from
Eleusis for demolition by Huzur
Gemi Sokum Ltd.

Wild Grebe looking particularly smart in P&O colours. *[FotoFlite incorporating Skyfotos]*

The Moroccan *Imouzzer* had numbers 2 and 3 hatches twinned, these were immediately forward and abaft of the superstructure. She has the usual union-purchase derricks, a fore topmast and the standard funnel design. *[Hans-Joachim Reinecke/David Whiteside collection]*

Imouzzer under Comninos control as *Tropicana Reefer*. *[David Whiteside collection]*

Yard No.87 **RAGNI BERG**
IMO 7710317 6,984/5,064g
4,060/2,707n 9,495d
144.74 x 135.21 x 18.01 x 11.64 metres
Refrigerated capacity: 398,312 cubic feet
Sulzer 6RND68 2SCSA oil engine by
A/S Horten Verft, Horten; 11,400 BHP,
21.5 knots.
7.8.1978: Launched for P/R Reeferberg
(Peter Y. Berg), Drammen, Norway as
RAGNI BERG.
11.1978: Completed
1983: Transferred to K/S Sea Reefer
Ltd. (Peter Y. Berg), Drammen).
1985: Owner and ship transferred to
Nassau, Bahamas.
1987: Renamed BAHAMIAN REEFER.
1988: Sold to Mediteranska Plovidba,
Korcula, Yugoslavia and renamed
OTRANT FRIGO.
1992: Transferred to Dulcina Shipping
Company, Panama Mediteranska
Plovidba, Korcula, Croatia, managers)
and transferred to St. Vincent and
Grenadines flag.
1993: Sold to Valeria Maritime S.A.,
Nassau (Target Marine S.A. [Tony
Comninos], Piraeus, Greece) and
renamed ADRIATIC TRADER.
1994: Sold to A/S Gerrards Rederi,
Kristiansand, Norway (Ugland Brothers
Ltd., Egham, Surrey) and renamed UB
POLARIS.
1997: Transferred to Ugland Reefers
Ltd. (Ugland International Holdings
Ltd.), George Town, Cayman Islands.
2002: Sold to Saudi Cold Storage Ltd.,
Jeddah, Saudi Arabia and renamed
TBREED III.
23.9.2003: Arrived Alang for
demolition.

Top: The second *Ragni Berg* has a lattice-topped funnel. Cargo gear is the usual union-purchase type, but there is no fore topmast. The ventilator trunks fitted to the hatches are non-standard. *[Fotoflite incorporating Skyfotos], 241589]*
Middle: *Ragni Berg* as *Adriatic Trader*. *[David Whiteside collection]*
Bottom: *Ragni Berg* now as *UB Polaris*. *[FotoFlite incorporating Skyfotos, 260505]*

Yard No.90 **RIO ESMERALDAS**
IMO 7809687 6,987/5,065g 4,060/2,705n 8040d
144.46 x 135.21 x 18.01 x 11.64 metres
Refrigerated capacity: 390,013 cubic feet
Sulzer 6RND68 2SCSA oil engine by A/S Horten
Verft, Horten; 11,400 BHP, 21 knots.
26. 3.1979: Launched for Flota Bananera
Ecuatoriana S.A., Guyaquil, Ecuador as RIO
ESMERALDAS.
31. 8.1979: Completed.
1989: Sold to Transportes Navieros Ecuatorianos
TRANSNAVE, Guayaquil and renamed ISLA
FERNANDINA.
1995: Sold to Omega Shipping Co. Ltd., Limassol,
Cyprus (International Reefer Services S.A. [Costas
Comninos], Piraeus, Greece) and renamed BALBOA
REEFER.
2002: Sold to Vision Shipholding Company,
Marshall Islands and renamed KIRKI.
2004: Sold to Nordic Cape Ltd., British Virgin
Isles (Ost-West Handel und Schiffahrt, Bremen,
Germany), renamed NORDIC CAPE and transferred
to St. Vincent and Grenadines flag.
12.8.2008: Arrived Alang for demolition.

This vessel had a chequered career. During March
1994, as *Isla Fernandina* she spent nine days
aground off Cartagena, Colombia during a voyage
from Guayaquil to Tripoli. As *Balboa Reefer* she
was rejected by charterers for loading bananas at
Ecuador in May 1999 after class withdrew her as
unsuitable due to generator failures. She was the
first vessel of the millennium to start a Panama Canal
transit on 1st January 2000 and on 16th May 2000
she was in collision with the bulker *Platitera* (IMO
7430682, 36,000/1976) after dragging her anchor off
La Plata, Argentina. She was detained at Portland
on 30th September 2000 by the Admiralty Marshall
on behalf of the crew in respect of unpaid wages and
again on 6th October 2000 by the British Maritime
and Coastguard Agency for various significant
deficiencies. She was detained for a total of 37 days.

Top: *Rio Esmeraldas.* [FotoFlite incorporating Skyfotos, 46694]
Middle: *Isla Fernandina.* [David Whiteside collection]
Bottom: *Balboa Reefer.* [FotoFlite incorporating Skyfotos, 179823]

Yard No. 91 **RIO CHONE**
IMO 7812634 6,976/5,064g
4,090/2,716n 9,300d
144.43 x 133.74 x 18.01 x 11.61 metres
Refrigerated capacity: 390,013 cubic feet
Sulzer 6RND68 2SCSA oil engine by A/S Horten Verft, Horten; 11,400 BHP, 21.5 knots.
1980: Completed for Flota Bananera Ecuatoriana S.A., Guayaquil, Ecuador as RIO CHONE.
1988: Sold to Transportes Navieros Ecuatorianos S.A. TRANSNAVE, Guayaquil and renamed ISLA GENOVESA.
1995: Sold to Orca Navigation Co. Ltd., Limassol, Cyprus (International Reefer Services S.A. [Costas Comninos], Piraeus, Greece and renamed MALIBU REEFER.
1999: Renamed MALICIA.
2000: Sold to Red Scorpio Shipping S.A., Panama (Eurotrust Holdings S.A., Piraeus) and renamed LILIA I.
2002: Sold to Bay Shipping S.A., Panama (Target Marine S.A. [A. Poulman and L. Papazis], Piraeus and renamed ARIADNE.
2003: Sold to Wharton Alliance Ltd., British Virgin Isles (Ost-West Handel und Schiffahrt, Bremen, Germany) and renamed NORDIC STAR and transferred to St. Vincent and Grenadines flag.
16.9.2008: Beached at Chittagong for demolition.

Top: *Rio Chone.* [FotoFlite incorporating Skyfotos, 4170]
Middle: *Isla Genovesa.* [David Whiteside collection]
Bottom: *Malibu Reefer.* [Hans-Joachim Reinecke/David Whiteside collection]

Yard No.93 **RIO PALORA**
IMO 7909798 6,975/5,064g 4,070/2,716n
9,888d
144.46 x 133.76 x 18.01 x 11.64 metres
Refrigerated capacity: 395,416 cubic feet
Sulzer 6RND68 2SCSA oil engine by A/S
Horten Verft, Horten; 11,400 BHP, 21.0 knots.
10.11.1980: Launched for Flota Bananera
Ecuatoriana S.A., Guayaquil, Ecuador as RIO
PALORA.
24.03.1981: Completed for Flota Bananera
Ecuatoriana S.A., Guyaquil as PAQUISHA.
1989: Sold to Transportes Navieros
Ecuatorianos S.A. TRANSNAVE, Guayaquil
and renamed ISLA ISABELA.
1995: Sold to Galgot Shipping Co. Ltd.,
Limassol, Cyprus (International Reefer
Services S.A. [Costas Comninos], Piraeus,
Greece) and renamed ORENOCO REEFER.
1999: Sold to Marshall Shipping S.A., Panama
(Eurotrust Holdings S.A., Piraeus) and
renamed RENO.
2002: Sold to Active Shipping S.A., Panama
and renamed ARMONIA.
2003: Sold to Bremerton Alliance Ltd., British
Virgin Isles (Ost-West Handel und Schiffahrt,
Bremen, Germany), renamed NORDIC ICE
and transferred to St. Vincent and Grenadines flag.
4.8.2008: Arrived Alang for demolition

Built by Haugesund M/V A/S, Haugesund.

Yard No.64 **ELISABETH BERG**
IMO 7710329 6,976/5,061g 4,079/2,720n
9.247d
144.43 x 135.21 x 18.01 x 11.64 metres
Refrigerated capacity: 395,240 cubic feet
Sulzer 6RND68 2SCSA oil engine by A/S
Horten Verft, Horten; 11,400 BHP, 21.0 knots.
22.5.1979: Launched for P/R Berfa (Peter Y.
Berg), Drammen, Norway as ELISABETH
BERG.

Top: The Ecuadorian *Isla Isabela*, ex *Rio Palora*. *[David Whiteside collection]*
Middle and bottom: Although the former *Rio Palora* had the name *Nordic Ice* only
for five years, she carried two distinctly different liveries, the white hull with a blue
band being reminiscent of troopship colours (middle), and with red hull (bottom).
[Both: FotoFlite incorporating Skyfotos, 276303 and 289177]

31.10.1979: Completed.
1981: Sold to the Government of the Republic of Iraq (Ministry of Agriculture, Agrarian Reform – State Fisheries Co.), Basrah, Iraq and renamed ZAIN AL-QAWS.
1987: Transferred to the Government of Iraq, State Enterprise for Water Transport, Baghdad, Iraq.
2001: Sold to Al Bakheet Gulf Establishment for Transport and Trading, Aqaba, Jordan and renamed JAWAHER
2003: Reported to have been scrapped in India.

Built by Kaldnes M/V A/S, Tonsberg

Yard No.214 **RIO BABAHOYO**
IMO 7909803 6,975/5,064g 4,070/2,716n 9,344d
144.46 x 133.76 x 18.01 x 11.64 metres
Refrigerated capacity: 390,013 cubic feet
Sulzer 6RND68 2SCSA oil engine by A/S Horten Verft, Horten; 11,400 BHP, 21.0 knots.
20.5.1980: Launched for Flota Bananera Ecuatoriana S.A., Guayaquil, Ecuador as RIO BABAHOYO
21. 8.1980: Completed.
1988: Sold to Transportes Navieros Ecuatorianos S.A. TRANSNAVE, Guayaquil and renamed ISLA PINTA.
1995: Sold to Sea Trophy Maritime Co. Ltd., Limassol, Cyprus (International Reefer Services S.A. [Costas Comninos], Piraeus, Greece) and renamed CURACAO REEFER.
2002: Sold to Lexite Marine S.A., Marshall Islands and renamed KALYPSO.
2003: Sold to Nordic Bay Ltd., British Virgin Isles (Ost-West Handel and Schiffahrt, Bremen, Germany), renamed NORDIC BAY and transferred to St. Vincent and Grenadines flag.
4.8.2008: Arrived Alang for demolition.

Zain Al-Qaws with Lauritzen-Peninsular Reefers markings on her lattice-topped funnel. The work boats on davits either side of the after mast house were added following her sale to Iraq. *[FotoFlite incorporating Skyfotos]*

The last Super Clipper, *Rio Babahoyo* as *Curacao Reefer* (above) and *Nordic Bay* (below). *[David Whiteside collection and FotoFlite incorporating Skyfotos, 307028]*

Elder Dempster in colour

Top: Colour views of the first post-war S class are rare. This is *Sherbro* at Avonmouth (see 'Record' 47, page 136). *[R.M. Parsons/J.D. Hill-Malcolm Cranfield collection]*
Middle: *Eboe* sails from Avonmouth on 14th February 1970 (see 'Record' 47, page 142). *[Ian Stockbridge/Malcolm Cranfield collection]*
Bottom: *Obuasi* arrives at Avonmouth on 18th July 1971 (see 'Record' 48, page 199). *[Malcolm Cranfield]*

Top: *Maldive Courage*, formerly the *Owerri*, at Singapore on 11th February 1982 (see 'Record' 48, page 199). *[Malcolm Cranfield collection]*

Middle: *Daru* in Guinea Gulf colours (see 'Record' 48, page 202). *[FotoFlite incorporating Skyfotos, 329761]*

Bottom: *Daru* as *Anjo One* at Singapore in March 1981, still with a buff funnel. *[Malcolm Cranfield collection]*

Top: A less than pristine *Fumurra*, formerly *Dumurra*, is assisted into Avonmouth on 4th August 1981 by the Cory tug *Pengarth* (see 'Record' 48, page 204). *[Malcolm Cranfield]*

Middle: *Donga* on 4th June 1967 in Canadian waters (see 'Record' 48, page 205). *[V.A. Young and L.A. Sawyer collection]*

Bottom: *Dumbaia* on the New Waterway in 1981, her colours unchanged despite her sale (see 'Record' 48, page 206). *[Malcolm Cranfield collection]*

Top: *Cam Azobe*, formerly *Fulani*, on the New Waterway on 19th June 1980 (see page 9). *[Les Ring/Malcolm Cranfield collection]*

Middle: *Falaba* (see page 8). *[FotoFlite incorporating Skyfotos, 257459]*

Bottom: Sale of *Freetown* saw her initially become *Panseptos* (see page 9), as which she is still in very good external condition. Her ultimate owners were London-based Greeks, A.S. Lemos and D.G. and G.D. Skinitis. *[FotoFlite incorporating Skyfotos/Roy Fenton collection]*

Fian (above) with an all-black hull (see page 11) and *Bhamo* at Avonmouth with grey masts (right) (see page 6). *[FotoFlite incorporating Skyfotos, 354935; R.M. Parsons/J.D. Hill-Malcolm Cranfield collection]*

FUNNEL AND FLAG OF GRAND UNION (SHIPPING) LTD.

See pages 30 onwards.
[J.L. Loughran]